film posters of the 70s

the essential movies of the decade

from the reel poster gallery collection

edited by tony nourmand and graham marsh

aurum press

First published in 1998 by
Aurum Press Limited
25 Bedford Avenue
London WC1B 3AT

A catalogue record for this book is available from the British Library.

ISBN 1 85410 585 X

Art direction and design by Graham Marsh
Page make-up by Trevor Gray

7 6 5
2006 2005 2004

Printed in Singapore by Kyodo

ACKNOWLEDGEMENTS

Richard Allen
Farhad Amirahmadi
Joe Burtis
Glyn Callingham
Tony Crawley
The Crew from the Island
Eon Productions
Leslie Gardner
Roxanna Hajiani
John Hazelton
Eric Jean-Baptiste
John Kisch
Bruce Marchant
June Marsh
Thomas Milne
Hamid Joseph Nourmand
Gabriele Pantucci
Ken Schacter
Philip Shalam
Daniel Strebin
Yasumasa Takahashi
X-Man

The Reel Poster Gallery
72 Westbourne Grove
London W2 5SH
Tel: +44 (0)20 7727 4488
Fax: +44 (0)20 7727 4499

Web Site: www.reelposter.com
Email: info@reelposter.com

contents

as american as apple pie

Looking back at the 70s it is the American films, more than those of any other country, which dominate my memories. Young directors like Francis Ford Coppola, Martin Scorsese and William Friedkin brought intelligent and creative films to the screen and there was also the explosive birth of the Blaxploitation and Disaster genres, while cop movies took on a whole new dimension.

As far as poster design went, the artwork became largely homogeneous across national boundaries. The campaign for *Jaws* (1975) clearly marked this new trend with the same American artwork appearing on posters in Britain, Japan, Spain, France, Italy and Germany. Among the few bucking this trend were the Eastern Europeans, who continued to create their own distinctive designs for non-domestic films, producing highly individualist artwork for films like *Jaws*, *Star Wars*, *Cabaret* and *The Conversation.*

At the same time the mainstream film poster had begun to play a smaller part in the cinematic promotion process as more attention was given to marketing films via television, radio and trailers. Despite this phenomenon, much of the imagery was powerful. In our selection we have chosen some special styles to complement the more commonly seen images, such as the rarely seen R-rated poster for *A Clockwork Orange* (1971) and the American poster used only for a special screening of *Get Carter* (1971).

In preparing this series of books, we make every effort to identify and credit the designers of the posters. This information is rarely easily obtainable, as film posters, particularly those from America and Britain, were generally designed by in-house studio artists who were seldom permitted to sign their work. Unfortunately even the studios did not record this information. Thus, although we do our best to gather and publish information on poster artists, regrettably it is not always possible.

What appears on the pages that follow is, as with *60s*, only a cross-section of the poster images of a decade which we hope will bring back memories.

TONY NOURMAND

M*A*S*H (1970)
US 41 × 27 in. (104 × 69 cm)
(World Première Poster)

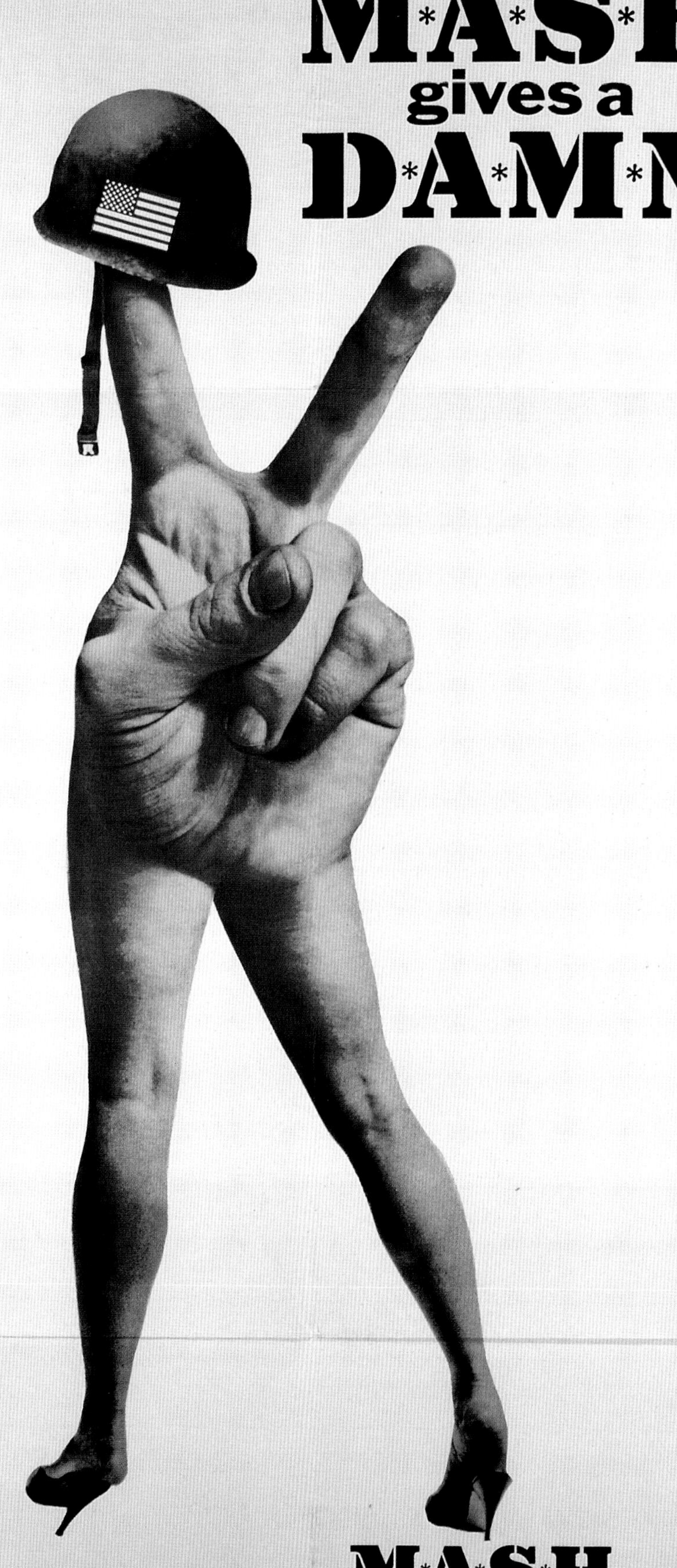
M*A*S*H
gives a
D*A*M*N
R
RESTRICTED-
Persons under
16 not admitted
UNLESS ACCOMPANIED
BY PARENT OR
ADULT GUARDIAN
20th Century-Fox presents M*A*S*H An Ingo Preminger Production
Starring DONALD SUTHERLAND · ELLIOTT GOULD · TOM SKERRITT
Co-Starring
SALLY KELLERMAN · ROBERT DUVALL · JO ANN PFLUG · RENE AUBERJONOIS
Produced by INGO PREMINGER Directed by ROBERT ALTMAN Screenplay by RING LARDNER, Jr. From a novel by RICHARD HOOKER Music by JOHNNY MANDEL PANAVISION®
COLOR by DeLuxe
WORLD PREMIERE SUNDAY, JANUARY 25TH THE Baronet
59th St. at 3rd Ave. · EL 5-1663-4
A WALTER READE THEATRE
PRINTED IN U.S.A.

clockwork oranges, deep throats

Pull back to reveal

A street in San Francisco. It's the bloody aftermath of a failed robbery.

Cut to

Detective Clint Eastwood, he is standing, gun in hand, over a cringing crook, and his words, when they come, are full of quiet menace.

EASTWOOD

'I know what you're thinking, punk. You're thinking did I fire six shots or only five? Now to tell you the truth, I've forgotten myself in all this excitement. But being this is a forty-four magnum, the most powerful handgun in the world and it'll blow your head clean off, you could ask yourself a question, "Do I feel lucky?!"...Well, **do** you, **punk**?'

Dirty Harry kicked off the decade with some memorable, much quoted dialogue of which Shakespeare, had he been a Hollywood screenwriter at the time, would have been proud. Although the Bard in all probability would have given Robert De Niro's 'You lookin' at me', speech from *Taxi Driver* to one of his assistants.

Somewhat unfairly, the legend that the 70s were 'the decade that style forgot' still persists, but every decade has its sartorial cross to bear. Indeed, some of the more dubious contemporary fashions even penetrated the sanctum of the Bond movies. Agent 007, who spent the 1960s in Savile Row suits, was now reincarnated as Roger Moore and saved the world in wingspan collared shirts, platform shoes, flares and a towelling leisure suit. Not even the ingenuity of 'Q' could come up with a gadget to keep Bond's wardrobe door shut until the 1970s had passed.

Some fashions, however, had an enormous impact with the 'in crowd'. Diane Keaton virtually invented thrift-shop cool when she starred in what is considered Woody Allen's best film, *Annie Hall*. The international fashion pack connected instantly with Keaton dressed in her baggy khaki pants, black waistcoat, white shirt and black tie with spots. An old tweed jacket and slouch hat completed the much copied 'Annie Hall' look of the late 70s. Annie Hall's catchphrase, 'Well, lah di dah!' could be heard whenever the fashionable gathered.

The immaculately suited and booted Michael Caine, playing a hard small-time South London gangster in the cult movie *Get Carter*, succeeds in angering an entire railway pub in Newcastle by ordering his bitter 'in a thin glass'. And after punching out a local racketeer, Caine tells him, in his inimitable deadpan voice, 'You're a big man, but you're out of shape, and I do this for a living'. Another hood, after having his sunglasses removed by Caine, is told that his eyes are like 'pissholes in the snow'. Alfie it isn't.

In the epic, multi-academy-award-winning *The Godfather*, Marlon Brando, his cheeks bulging with Kleenex, made offers that couldn't be refused. It was the 1970s equivalent of *Gone With The Wind* set to Nino Rota's evocative music. It was also a good career move for Diane Keaton, Al Pacino, James Caan and Robert Duvall who consequently got offers that they did not refuse.

The profits of dry cleaners soared as every week wannabe John Travoltas brought in their white suits to be cleaned after seeing their hero strut his stuff in *Saturday Night Fever*. Disco fever infected everyone, some people eventually recovered while others, to this day, leap to the floor and strike a pose whenever the sound of the Bee Gees starts up.

Classical film music was also never the same after Joseph Conrad's novel *Heart Of Darkness* metamorphosed into Coppola's *Apocalypse Now*. The controversial Vietnam war epic came complete with Wagner's Ride of the Valkyries blasting out of speakers strapped to Huey helicopter gunships. Robert Duvall as Lieutenant-Colonel Kilgore sniffing napalm and wasting an entire village because 'Charlie don't surf', added to the surreal, mesmerizing quality of the Oscar-winning movie.

Back in the real world the Bridge and Tunnel set queued for hours in New York's Times Square to see *Deep Throat*. Never mind the bad print, scrambled soundtrack and thin storyline, just sit back and see Linda Lovelace swallow her pride. And after audiences had seen *Last Tango In Paris*, 'pass the butter' took on a whole new meaning. Porno-chic had arrived.

Jack Nicholson was the main contender for the title of the 70s 'baddest bad-ass'. His portrayal of fiesty misfit Randle Patrick McMurphy, decked out in a worn leather jacket, workshirt and woollen hat trying to buck the system of a mental institution in Milos Foreman's *One Flew Over The Cuckoo's Nest*, won him an Oscar. But the number one film of the decade has to be director Bob Rafelson's *Five Easy Pieces*. Jack the Lad ordering his sandwich in a fast food joint was the 70s rarest groove.

Hippest on the block was Elliott Gould as Philip Marlowe in Robert Altman's *The Long Goodbye*. Operating in contemporary Los Angeles, circa 1973, Gould wore a dark, back-dated conservative off-the-peg J.C. Penny suit, white shirt and sober tie, the rest wore Kaftans and groovy cheese cloth threads. Marlowe's cat wore his own feline coat but insisted on a specific brand of cat food. When Marlowe was out of town on business the lucky cat got looked after by some Yoga-practicing, topless hippy chicks. Crazy ladies.

The domination of American films during the 1970s was increasingly reflected in the posters. With the exception of Poland and some other Eastern European countries the days of 'home-grown' poster art were numbered. American images were simply adapted to suit the relevant foreign markets. This made it easier for the boys back in the Stateside studios who handed out the marketing menus to hungry distributors, it went something like this: 'I'll have a large *Star Wars* with lobby cards, a side order of movie programmes and some Coke with ice for the projectionist.'

This arrangement was neatly summed up by the song title of a post-Panther, early 70s Soul Band called The Dramatics who sang 'Whatcha See Is Whatcha Get'.

GRAHAM MARSH

Get Carter (1971)
US 41 × 27 in. (104 × 69 cm)
(Special)
Design by John Van Hamersveld
Art Director: Mike Kaplan

MICHAEL CAINE
GET CARTER
R RESTRICTED Under 17 requires accompanying Parent or Adult Guardian
A MICHAEL KLINGER PRODUCTION STARRING MICHAEL CAINE in "GET CARTER" Co-Starring IAN HENDRY · JOHN OSBORNE and BRITT EKLAND
Screenplay by MIKE HODGES · Based on the novel "JACK'S RETURN HOME" by TED LEWIS · Produced by MICHAEL KLINGER · Directed by MIKE HODGES · IN METROCOLOR
A METRO-GOLDWYN-MAYER RELEASE

Five Easy Pieces (1970)
US 41 × 27 in. (104 × 69 cm)

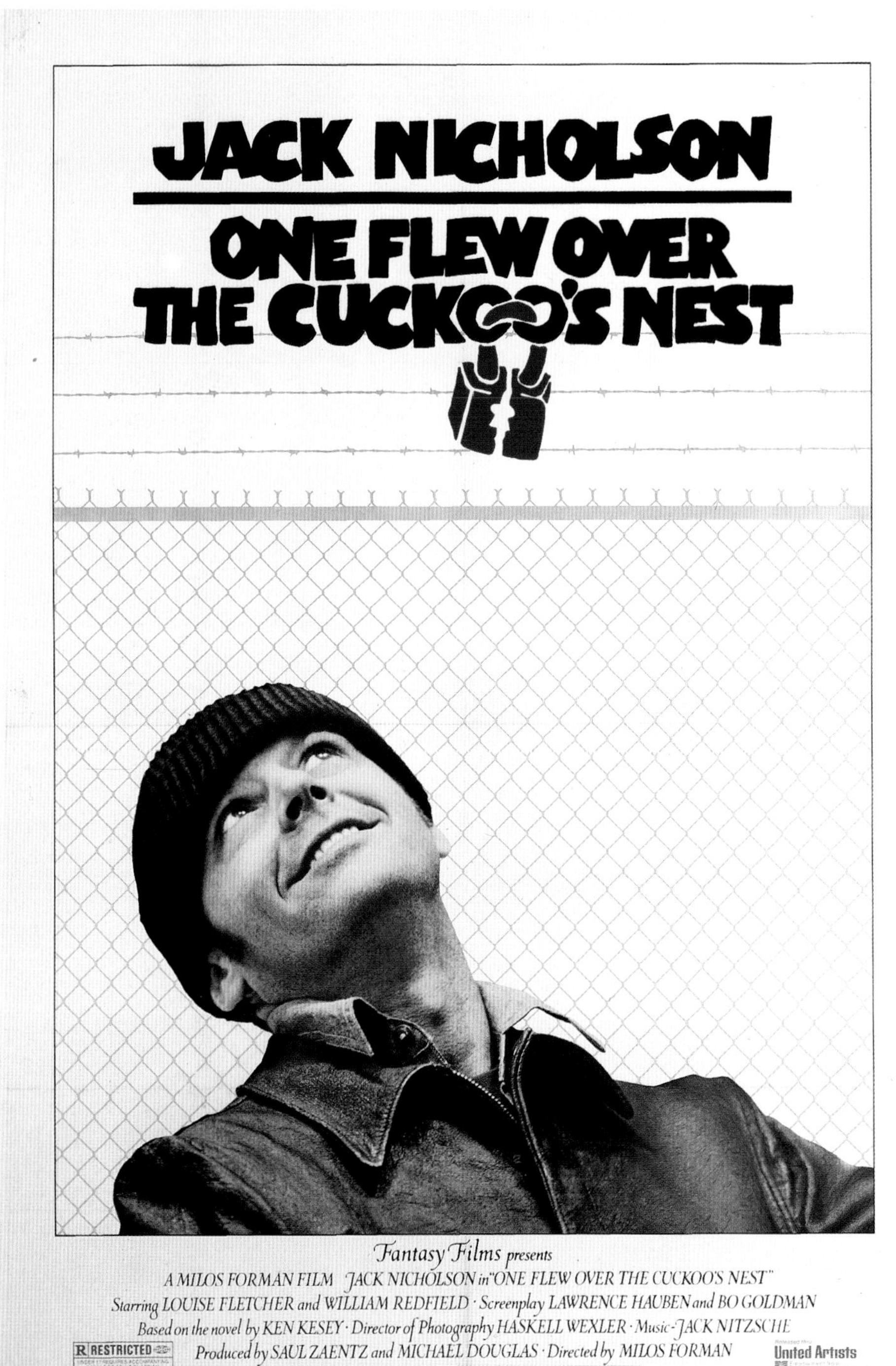

One Flew Over The Cuckoo's Nest (1975)
US 41 × 27 in. (104 × 69 cm)

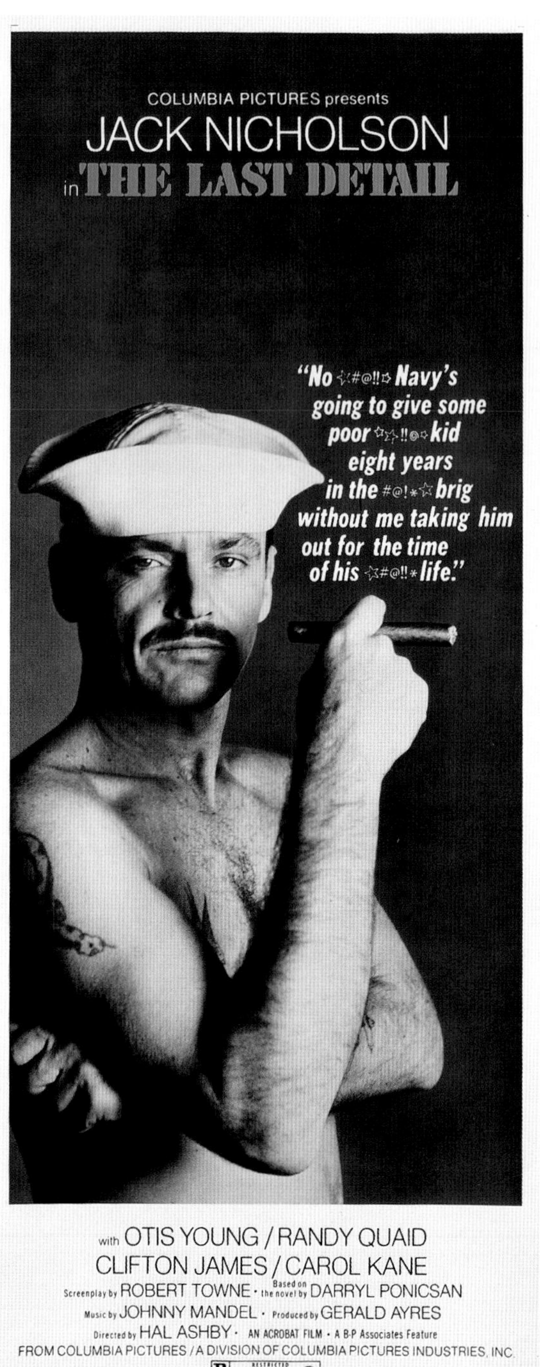

The Last Detail (1973)
US 36 × 14 (91 × 36 cm)

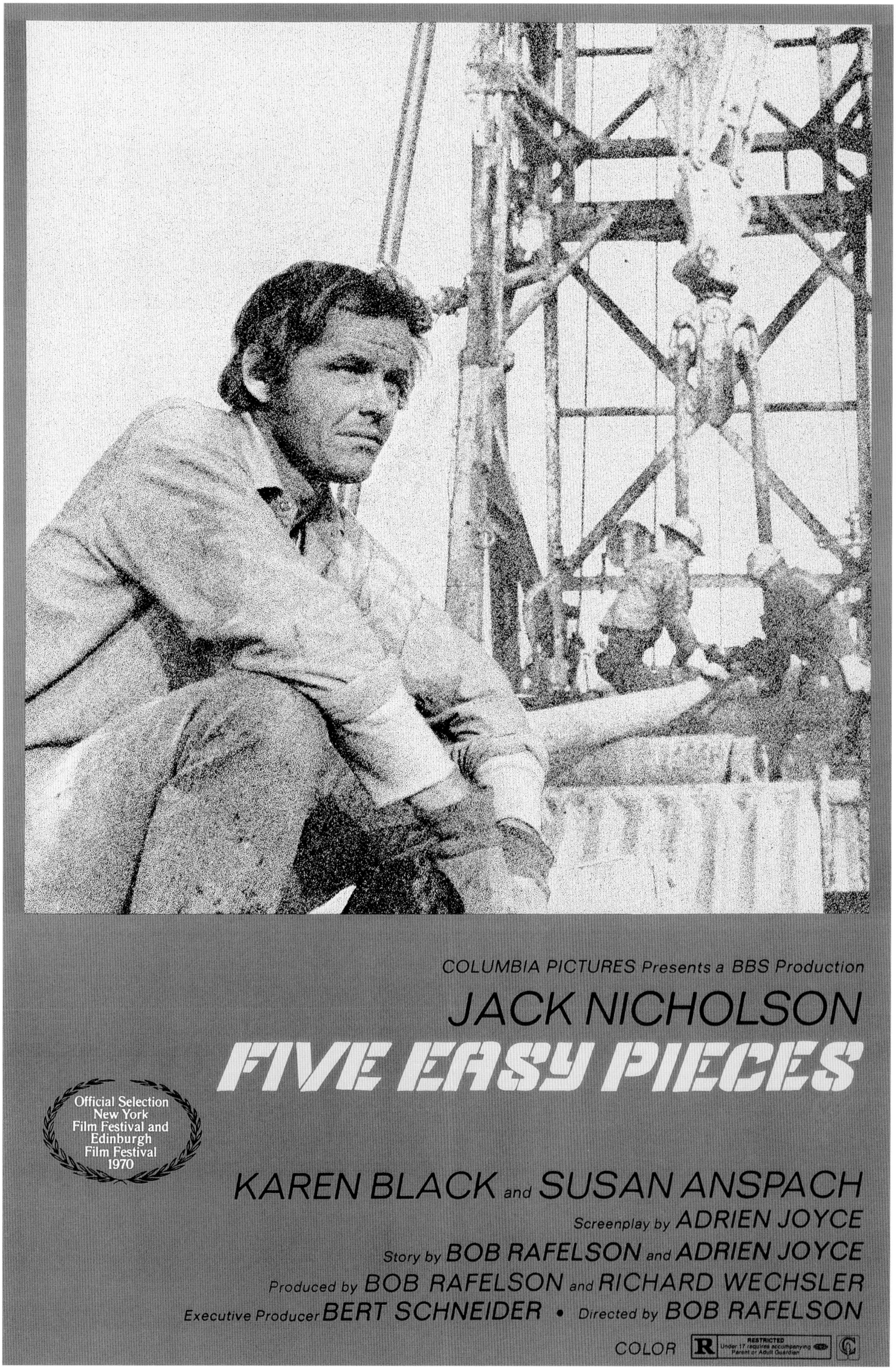

COLUMBIA PICTURES Presents a BBS Production

JACK NICHOLSON

FIVE EASY PIECES

Official Selection
New York
Film Festival and
Edinburgh
Film Festival
1970

KAREN BLACK and SUSAN ANSPACH

Screenplay by ADRIEN JOYCE

Story by BOB RAFELSON and ADRIEN JOYCE

Produced by BOB RAFELSON and RICHARD WECHSLER

Executive Producer BERT SCHNEIDER • Directed by BOB RAFELSON

COLOR 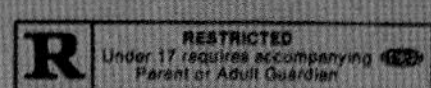

Chinatown (1974)
US 41 × 27 in. (104 × 69 cm)
Art by Jim Pearsall

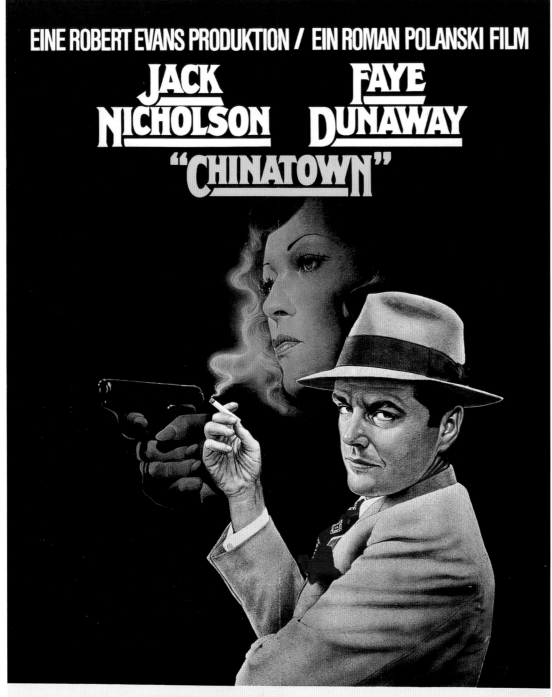

Chinatown (1974)
German 33 × 23 in. (84 × 58 cm)
Art by Richard Amsel

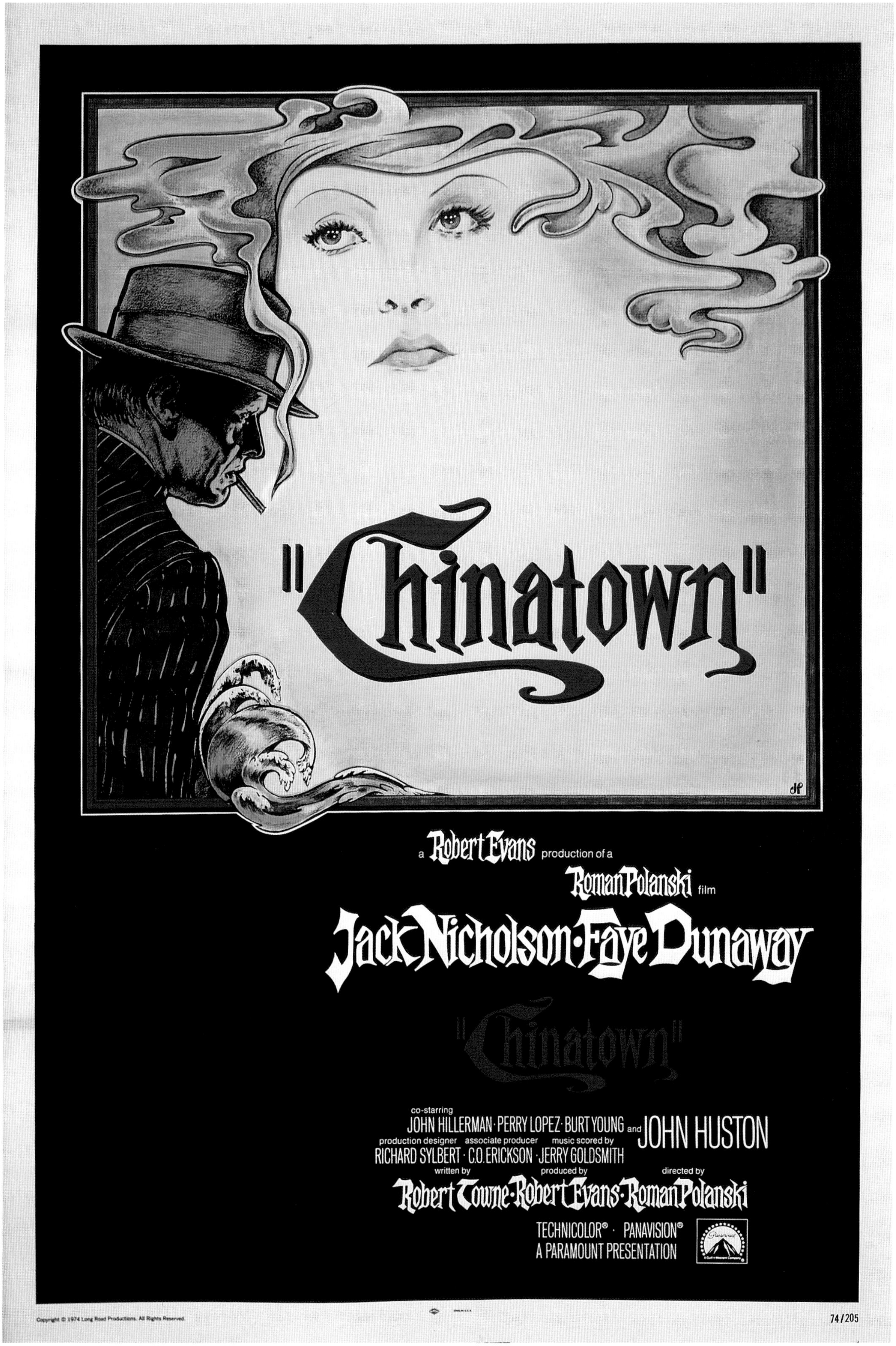

"Chinatown"

a Robert Evans production of a
Roman Polanski film

Jack Nicholson · Faye Dunaway

"Chinatown"

co-starring
JOHN HILLERMAN · PERRY LOPEZ · BURT YOUNG and JOHN HUSTON

production designer RICHARD SYLBERT · associate producer C.O. ERICKSON · music scored by JERRY GOLDSMITH

written by Robert Towne · produced by Robert Evans · directed by Roman Polanski

TECHNICOLOR® · PANAVISION®
A PARAMOUNT PRESENTATION

74/205

Magnum Force (1973)
US 36 × 14 in. (91 × 36 cm)
Design by Bill Gold

Clint
Eastwood
is Dirty Harry in
Magnum
Force

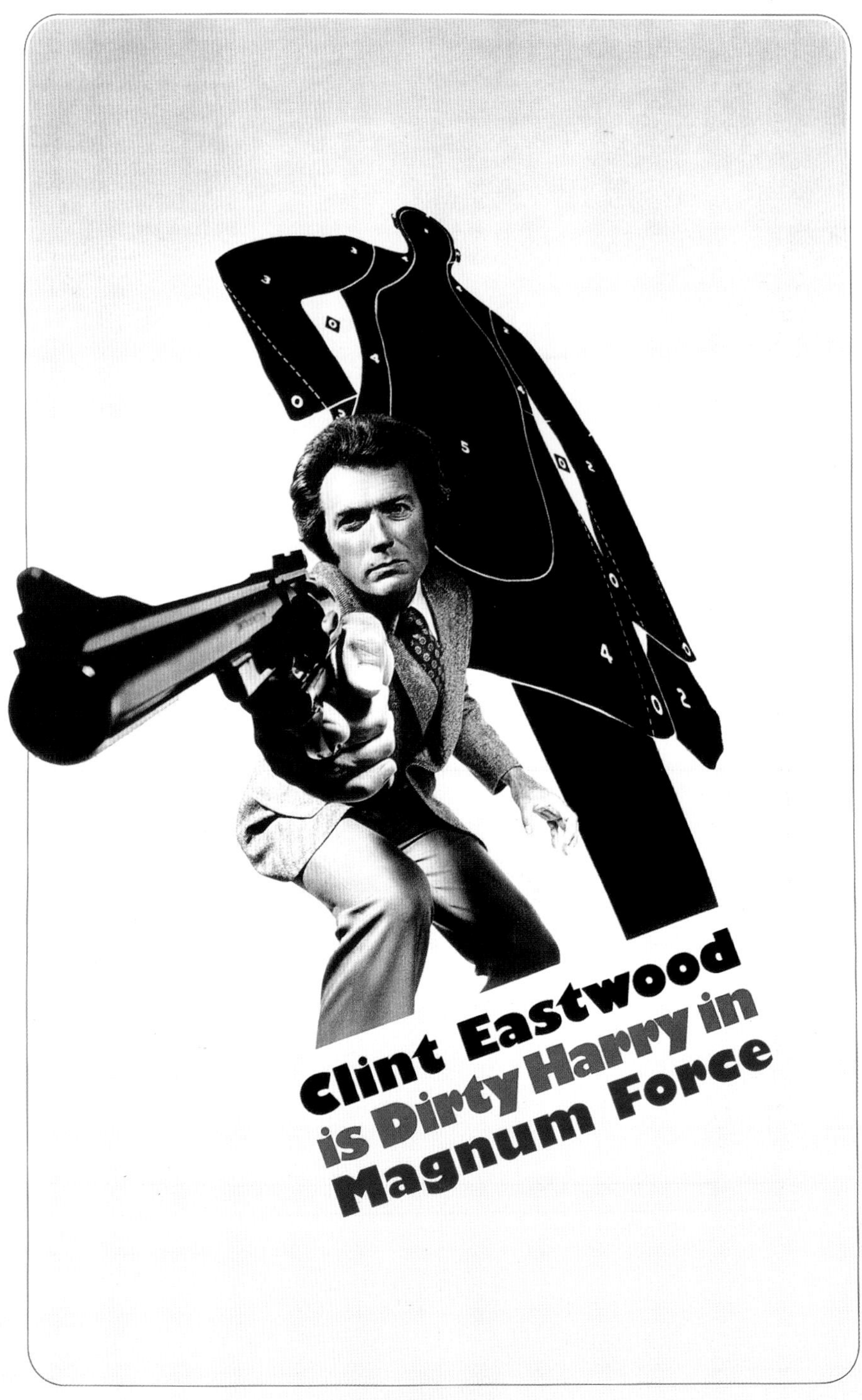

A MALPASO COMPANY FILM · Also Starring HAL HOLBROOK Co-Starring MITCHELL RYAN · DAVID SOUL · FELTON PERRY · ROBERT URICH · Music: LALO SCHIFRIN · Story by JOHN MILIUS · Screenplay by JOHN MILIUS and MICHAEL CIMINO · Produced by ROBERT DALEY · Directed by TED POST · PANAVISION® TECHNICOLOR® · Celebrating Warner Bros. 50th Anniversary · A Warner Communications Company R RESTRICTED Under 17 requires accompanying Parent or Adult Guardian

COPYRIGHT © 1973 WARNER BROS., INC. 73/318

Magnum Force (1973)
US 41 × 27 in. (104 × 69 cm)
Design by Bill Gold

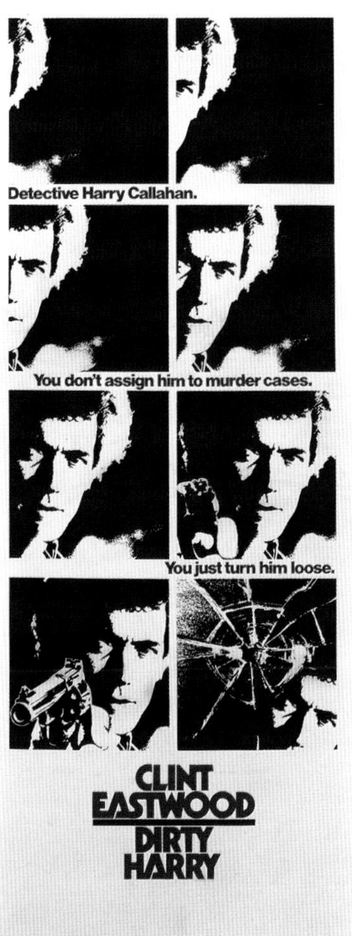

Detective Harry Callahan.
You don't assign him to murder cases.
You just turn him loose.
CLINT EASTWOOD
DIRTY HARRY

Dirty Harry (1971)
US 36 × 14 in. (91 × 36 cm)

Dirty Harry (1971)
US 41 × 27 in. (104 × 69 cm)

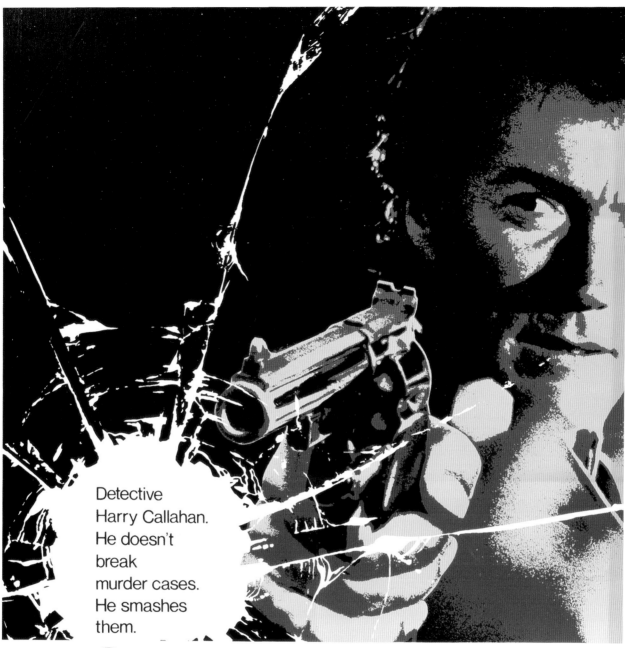

Detective
Harry Callahan.
He doesn't
break
murder cases.
He smashes
them.

Clint Eastwood
Dirty Harry

CLINT EASTWOOD in "DIRTY HARRY" A Malpaso Company Production Co-Starring HARRY GUARDINO • RENI SANTONI • ANDY ROBINSON • JOHN LARCH and JOHN VERNON as "The Mayor" • Executive Producer Robert Daley • Screenplay by Harry Julian Fink & R. M. Fink and Dean Reisner Story by Harry Julian Fink & R. M. Fink • Produced and Directed by Don Siegel • PANAVISION® • TECHNICOLOR® • Warner Bros., A Kinney Company

R RESTRICTED Under 17 Requires Accompanying Parent or Adult Guardian

71/349

The Taking Of Pelham One Two Three (1974)
British 30 × 40 in. (76 × 102 cm)

Serpico (1973)
US 41 × 27 in. (104 × 69 cm)

Many of his fellow officers considered him
the most dangerous man alive
-an honest cop.

A PARAMOUNT RELEASE
DINO DE LAURENTIIS
presents

AL PACINO in
"SERPICO"

Produced by MARTIN BREGMAN Directed by SIDNEY LUMET
Screenplay by WALDO SALT and NORMAN WEXLER Based on the book by PETER MAAS
Music by MIKIS THEODORAKIS Color by TECHNICOLOR® A Paramount Release

Original Soundtrack Album on Paramount Records and Tapes

74/13

"SERPICO"

The Godfather (1972)
British 41 x 27 in. (104 x 69 cm)

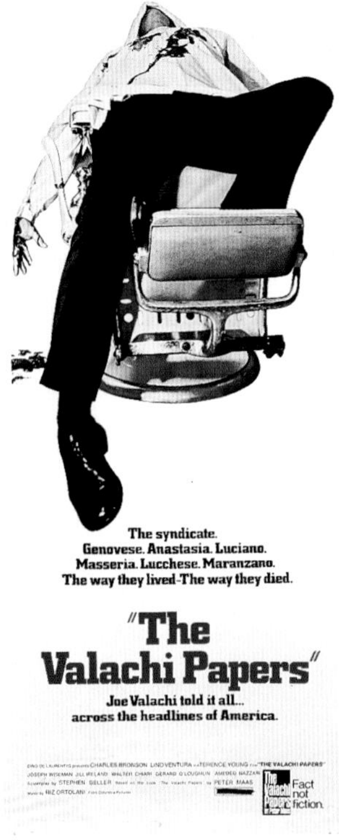

The Valachi Papers (1972)
US 36 × 14 in. (91 × 36 cm)

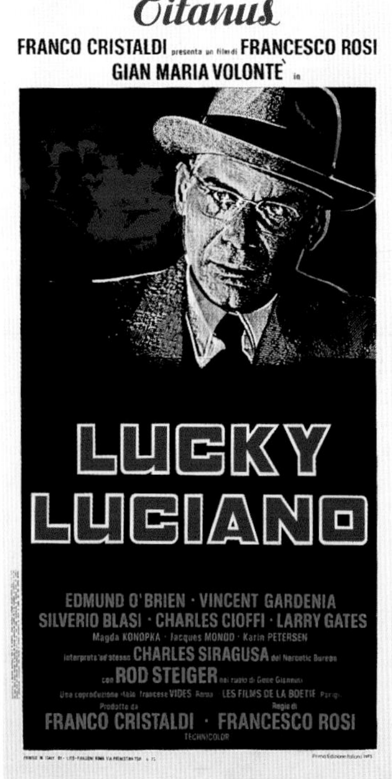

Lucky Luciano (1974)
Italian 28 × 13 in. (71 × 33 cm)

Mean Streets (1973)
US 41 × 27 in. (104 × 69 cm)

AN
Albert S. Ruddy
PRODUCTION

STARRING Marlon Brando
AND
Al Pacino James Caan Richard Castellano Robert Duvall
Sterling Hayden John Marley Richard Conte Diane Keaton

PRODUCED BY Albert S. Ruddy DIRECTED BY Francis Ford Coppola SCREENPLAY BY Mario Puzo AND Francis Ford Coppola
BASED ON Mario Puzo's NOVEL "The Godfather" MUSIC SCORED BY Nino Rota Color By Technicolor® A Paramount Picture

Distributed by Cinema International Corporation SOUNDTRACK ALBUM AVAILABLE ON PARAMOUNT RECORDS

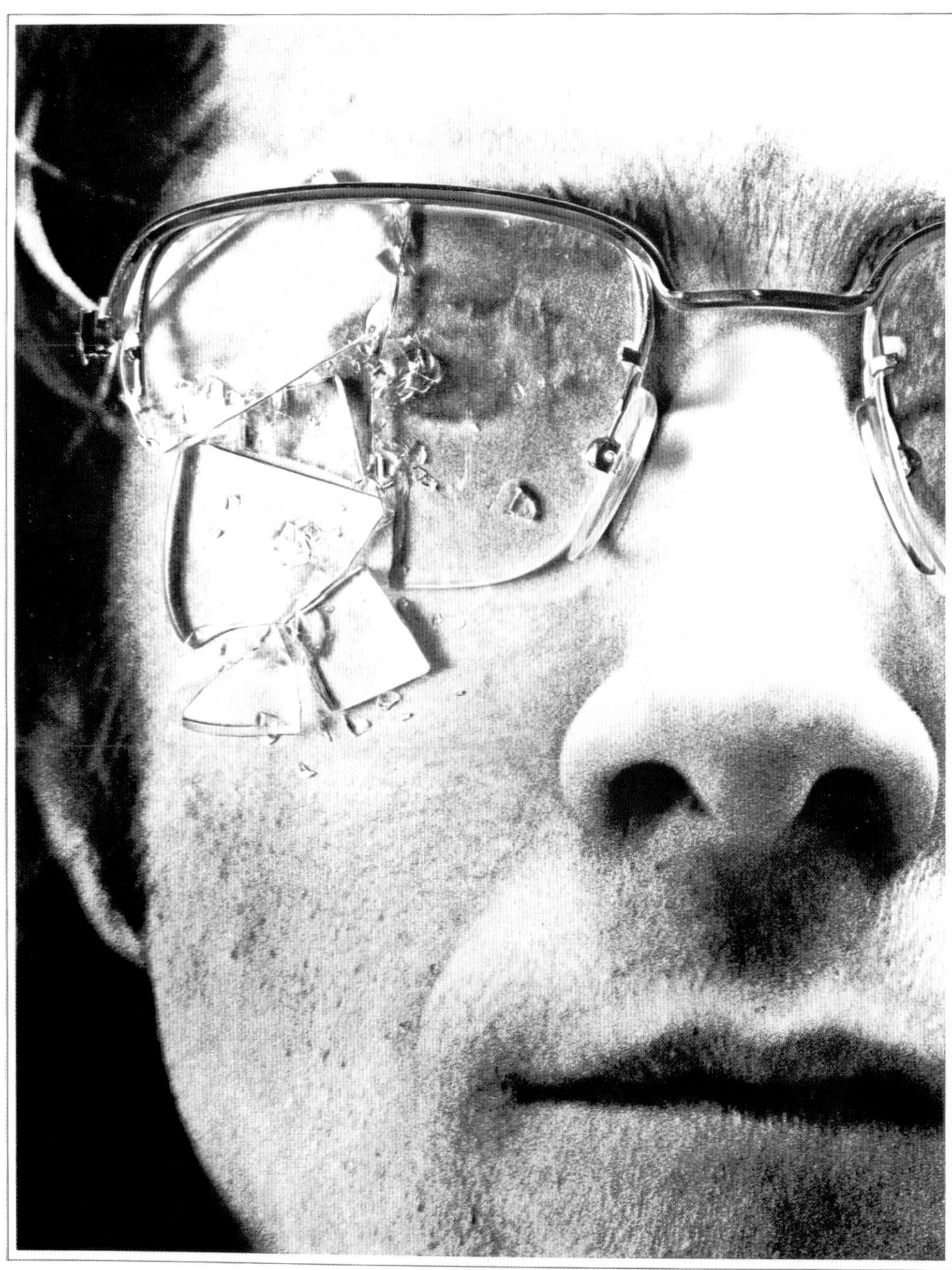

Straw Dogs (1971)
US 41 × 27 in. (104 × 69 cm)

Death Wish (1974)
US 41 × 27 in. (104 × 69 cm)

Vigilante, city style – judge, jury, and executioner.

A Paramount Release
DINO DE LAURENTIIS Presents

CHARLES BRONSON

in a **MICHAEL WINNER** film

"DEATH WISH"

Co-starring **VINCENT GARDENIA WILLIAM REDFIELD** and **HOPE LANGE** Music by **HERBIE HANCOCK**
from the novel **"DEATH WISH"** by **BRIAN GARFIELD** Screenplay by **WENDELL MAYES**
Produced by **HAL LANDERS** and **BOBBY ROBERTS** Directed and Co-Produced by **MICHAEL WINNER**

R

TECHNICOLOR® A Paramount Release

74/225

"DEATH WISH"

The French Connection (1971)
US 41 × 27 in. (104 × 69 cm)

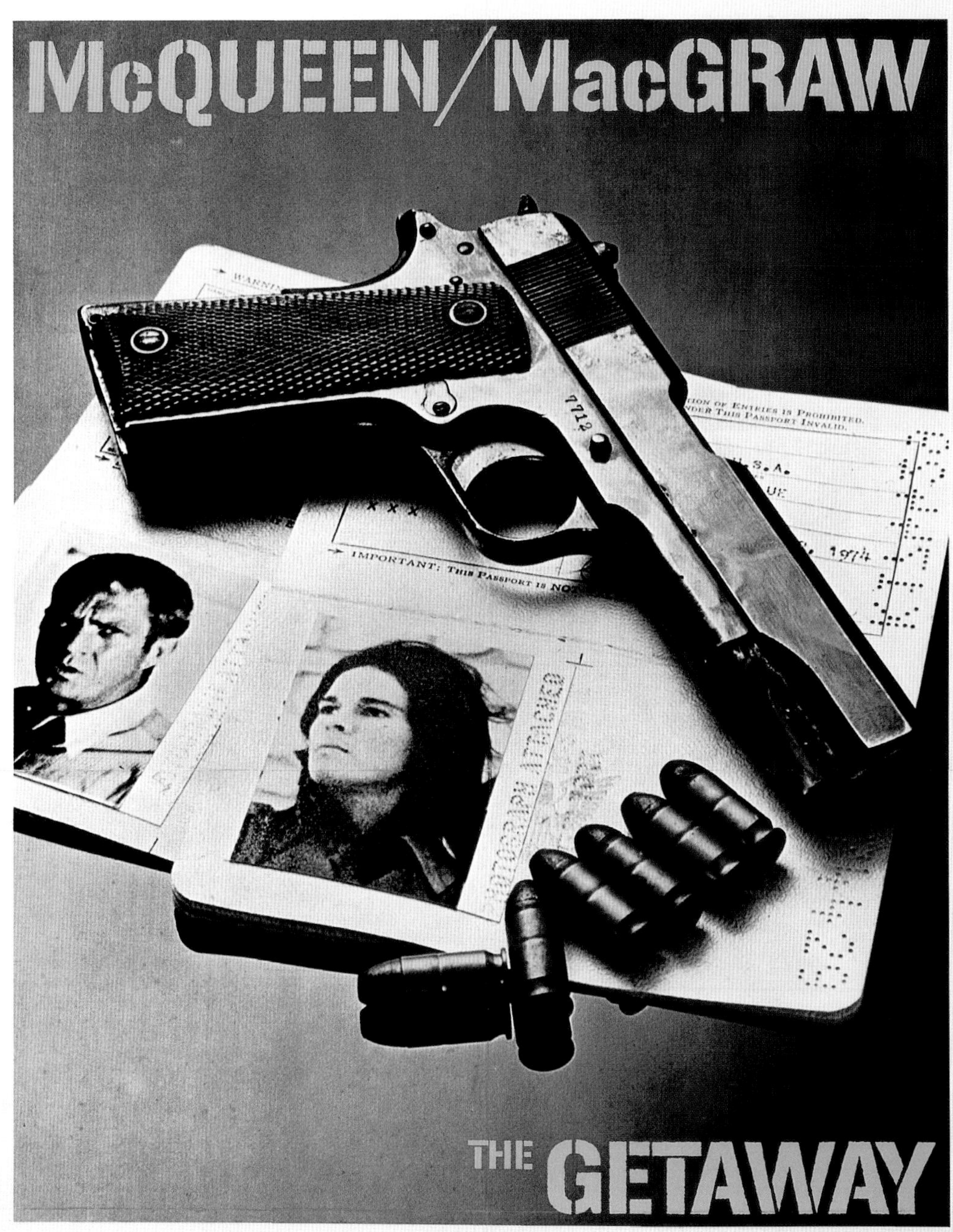

McQUEEN/MacGRAW
THE GETAWAY
STEVE McQUEEN/ALI MacGRAW IN "THE GETAWAY" A FIRST ARTISTS PRESENTATION · CO-STARRING BEN JOHNSON · AL LETTIERI AND SALLY STRUTHERS AS "FRAN" · SCREENPLAY BY WALTER HILL · FROM THE NOVEL BY JIM THOMPSON · MUSIC BY QUINCY JONES
A SOLAR/FOSTER-BROWER PRODUCTION · PRODUCED BY DAVID FOSTER AND MITCHELL BROWER · DIRECTED BY SAM PECKINPAH
FILMED IN TODD-AO 35 · TECHNICOLOR® · A NATIONAL GENERAL PICTURES RELEASE
PG
PARENTAL GUIDANCE SUGGESTED

The Getaway (1972)
US 41 × 27 in. (104 × 69 cm)

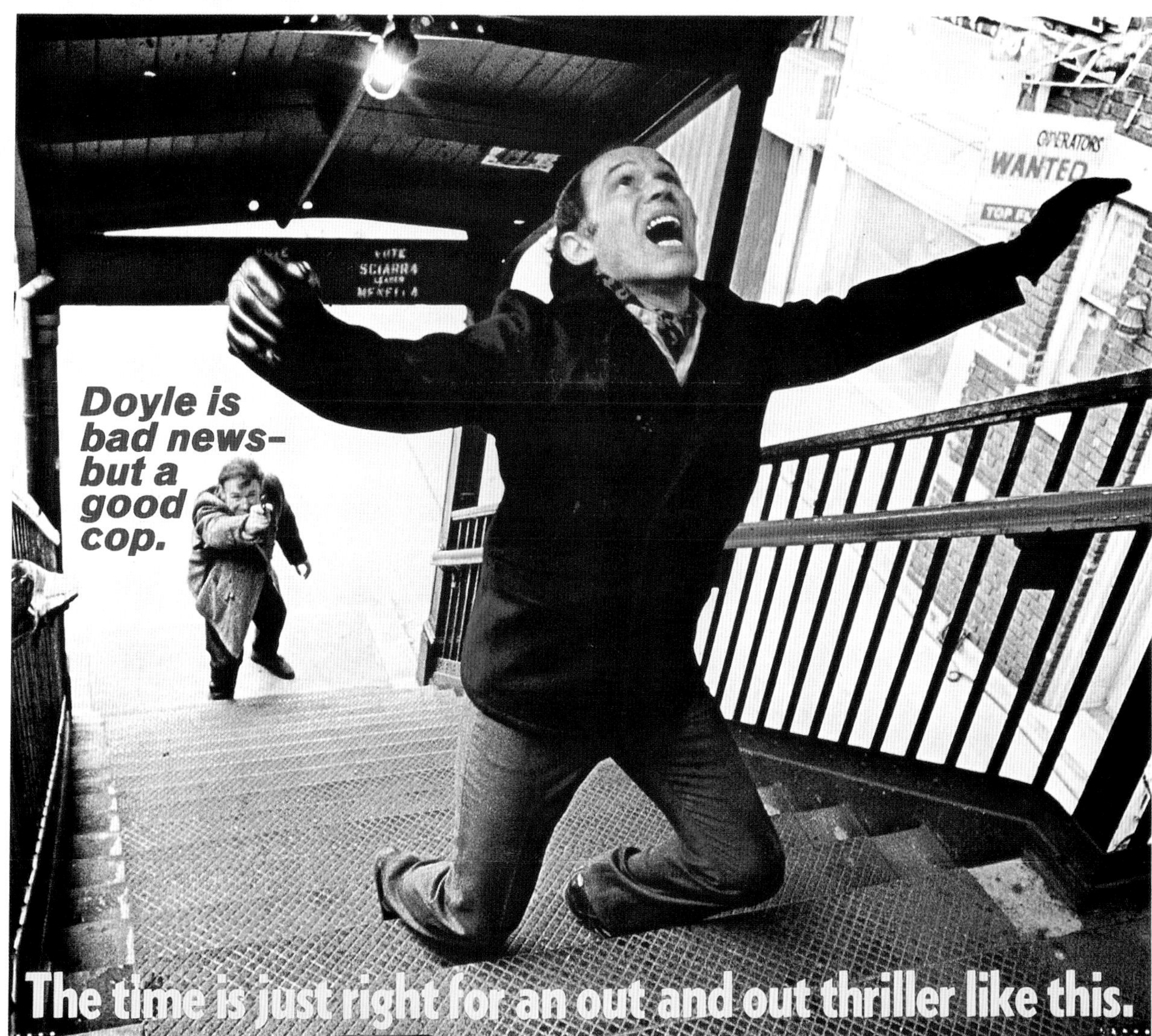

OPERATORS
WANTED
Doyle is bad news– but a good cop.
The time is just right for an out and out thriller like this.

THE FRENCH CONNECTION

20TH CENTURY-FOX PRESENTS "THE FRENCH CONNECTION" A PHILIP D'ANTONI PRODUCTION
STARRING GENE HACKMAN FERNANDO REY ROY SCHEIDER TONY LO BIANCO MARCEL BOZZUFFI
DIRECTED BY WILLIAM FRIEDKIN PRODUCED BY PHILIP D'ANTONI ASSOCIATE PRODUCER KENNETH UTT
EXECUTIVE PRODUCER G.DAVID SCHINE SCREENPLAY BY ERNEST TIDYMAN MUSIC COMPOSED AND CONDUCTED BY DON ELLIS
COLOR BY DE LUXE®

71/316

The Long Goodbye (1973)
US 36 × 14 in. (91 × 36 cm)
(Style B)
Art attributed to Richard Amsel

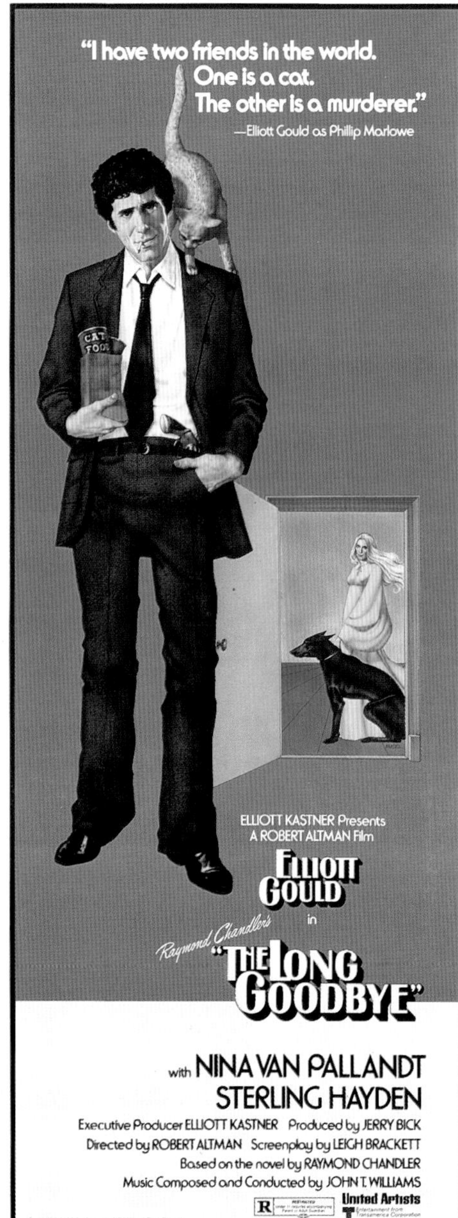

The Long Goodbye (1973)
US 36 × 14 in. (91 × 36 cm)
Art by Richard Amsel

The Long Goodbye (1973)
US International
36 × 14 in. (91 × 36 cm)

The Long Goodbye (1973)
US 41 × 27 in. (104 × 69 cm)
Art by Jack Davis

ELLIOTT KASTNER presents A ROBERT ALTMAN Film

ELLIOTT GOULD in "THE LONG GOODBYE"

with NINA VAN PALLANDT · STERLING HAYDEN

Executive Producer ELLIOTT KASTNER · Produced by JERRY BICK · Directed by ROBERT ALTMAN · Screenplay by LEIGH BRACKETT

R RESTRICTED Under 17 requires accompanying Parent or Adult Guardian

Based on the novel by RAYMOND CHANDLER · Music Composed and Conducted by JOHN T. WILLIAMS **United Artists**

STYLE C

73/63

Un Flic / (Dirty Money) (1972)
French 31 × 24 in. (79 × 61 cm)
Art by René Ferracci

The Driver (1978)
US 41 × 27 in. (104 × 69 cm)
Art by M. Daily

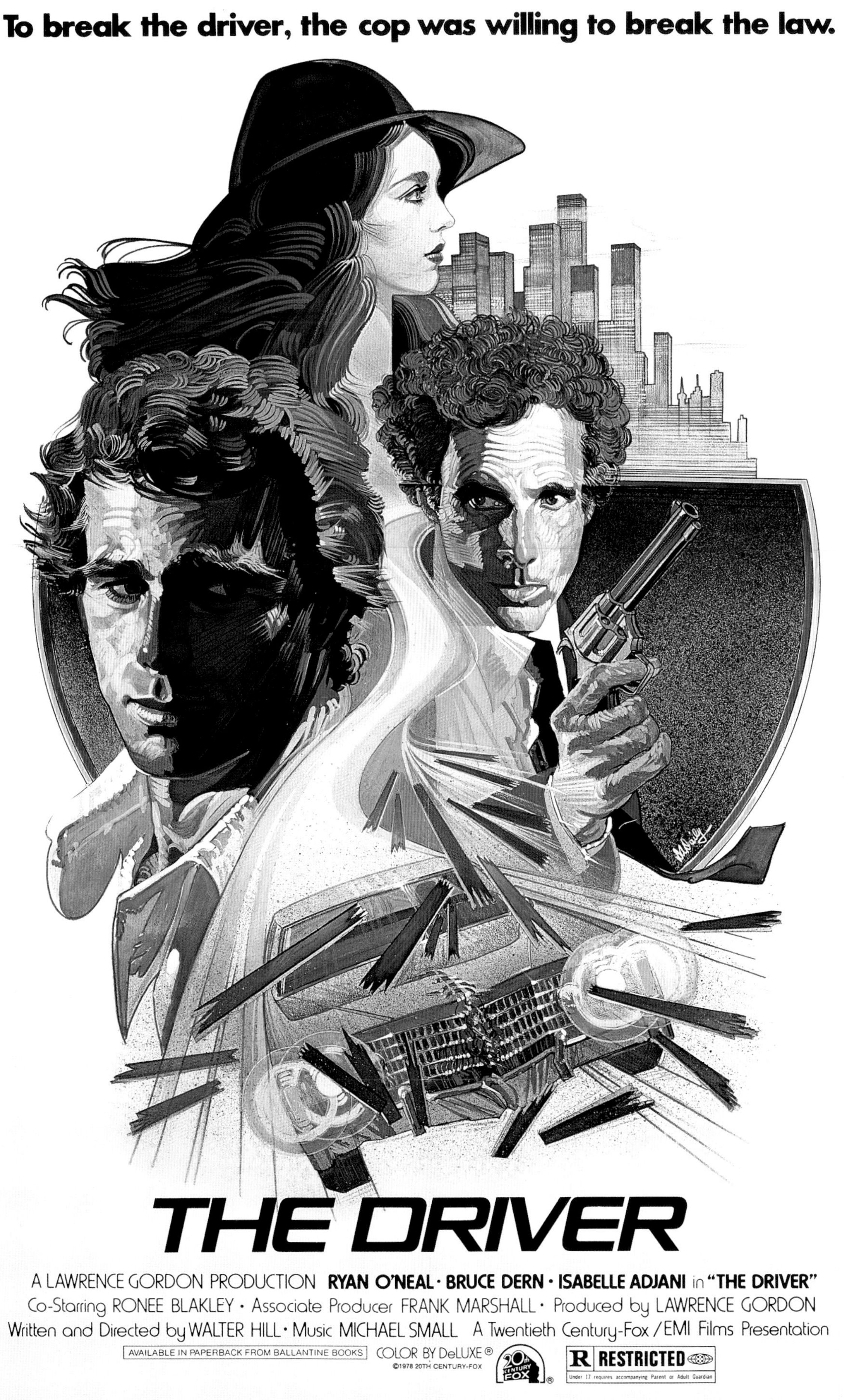

To break the driver, the cop was willing to break the law.
THE DRIVER
A LAWRENCE GORDON PRODUCTION RYAN O'NEAL · BRUCE DERN · ISABELLE ADJANI in "THE DRIVER"
Co-Starring RONEE BLAKLEY · Associate Producer FRANK MARSHALL · Produced by LAWRENCE GORDON
Written and Directed by WALTER HILL · Music MICHAEL SMALL A Twentieth Century-Fox / EMI Films Presentation
AVAILABLE IN PAPERBACK FROM BALLANTINE BOOKS
COLOR BY DeLUXE®
©1978 20TH CENTURY-FOX
R RESTRICTED
Under 17 requires accompanying Parent or Adult Guardian

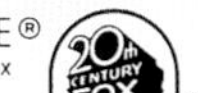

Two-Lane Blacktop (1971)
US 41 × 27 in. (104 × 69 cm)

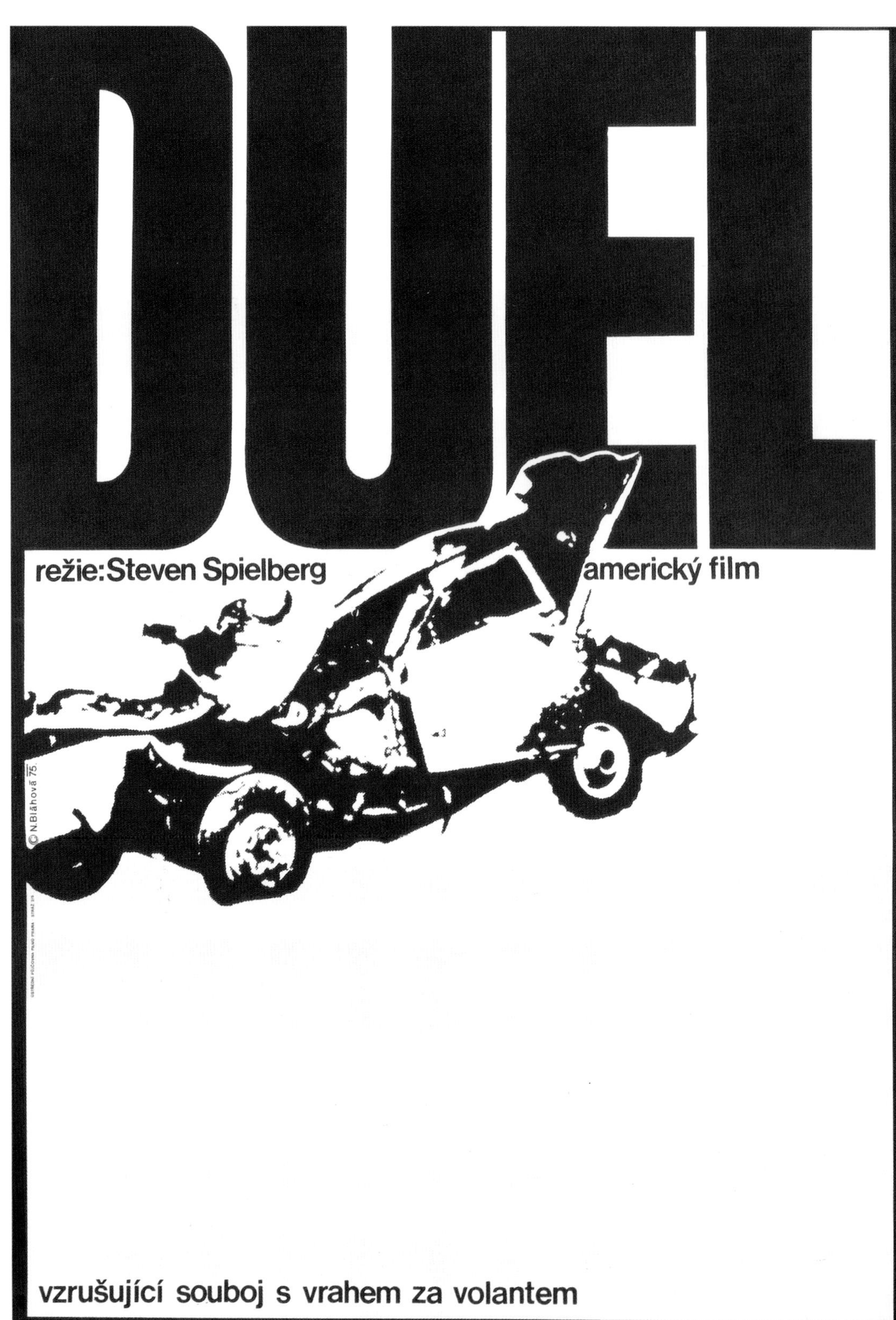

Duel (1971)
Czech 33 × 23 in. (84 × 58 cm)
Art by N. Blahova

JAMES TAYLOR IS THE DRIVER
WARREN OATES IS GTO
LAURIE BIRD IS THE GIRL
DENNIS WILSON IS THE MECHANIC

TWO-LANE BLACKTOP
IS THE PICTURE

TWO-LANE BLACK-TOP

JAMES TAYLOR · WARREN OATES · LAURIE BIRD · DENNIS WILSON

Screenplay by RUDOLPH WURLITZER and WILL CORRY • Story by WILL CORRY • Directed by MONTE HELLMAN • Produced by MICHAEL S. LAUGHLIN

A MICHAEL S. LAUGHLIN PRODUCTION • A UNIVERSAL PICTURE • TECHNICOLOR® R RESTRICTED Under 17 requires accompanying Parent or Adult Guardian

71/262

Vanishing Point (1970)
US 41 × 27 in. (104 × 69 cm)

On Any Sunday (1971)
US 41 × 27 in. (104 × 69 cm)
Photograph by John Bechtold

Le Mans (1971)
Japanese 60 × 20 in. (152 × 51 cm)

Tighten your seat belt.
You never had a trip like this before.

Hear the supercharged sounds of
DELANEY & BONNIE & FRIENDS
MOUNTAIN
JERRY REED
BIG MAMA THORNTON
THE DOUG DILLARD EXPEDITION
KIM & DAVE

VANISHING POINT

20th Century-Fox presents

BARRY NEWMAN in VANISHING POINT A CUPID PRODUCTION co starring DEAN JAGGER and Tony Award Winner CLEAVON LITTLE as Super Soul

produced by NORMAN SPENCER directed by RICHARD C. SARAFIAN screenplay by GUILLERMO CAIN Executive Producer MICHAEL PEARSON COLOR BY DE LUXE®

Original soundtrack available on Amos Records

GP ALL AGES ADMITTED Parental Guidance Suggested

71/49

Death Race 2000 (1975)
British 30 × 40 in. (76 × 102 cm)
Art by Tom William Chantrell

Mad Max (1979)
US 41 × 27 in. (104 × 69 cm)

80029

"MAD MAX"

The Warriors (1979)
US 41 × 27 in. (104 × 69 cm)
Art by Jarais

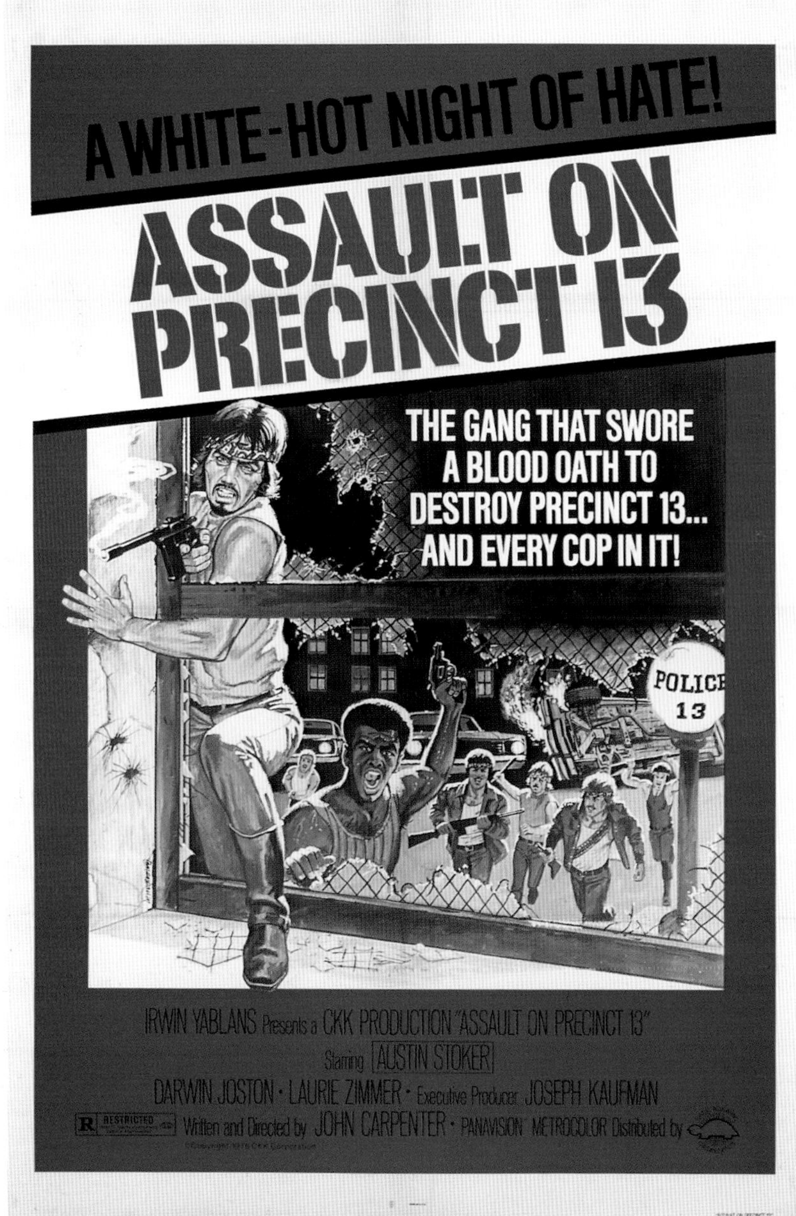

Assault On Precinct 13 (1976)
US 41 × 27 in. (104 × 69 cm)

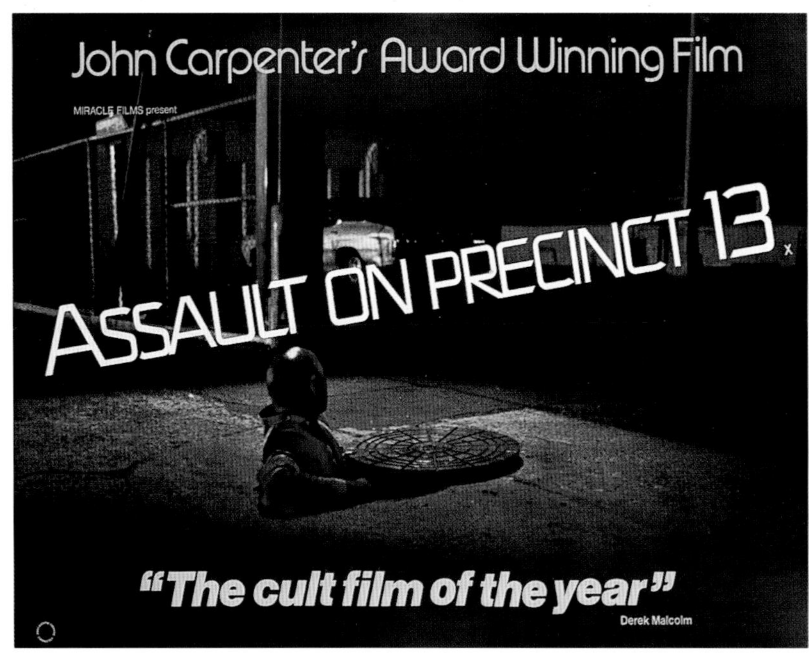

Assault On Precinct 13 (1976)
British 30 × 40 in. (76 × 102 cm)

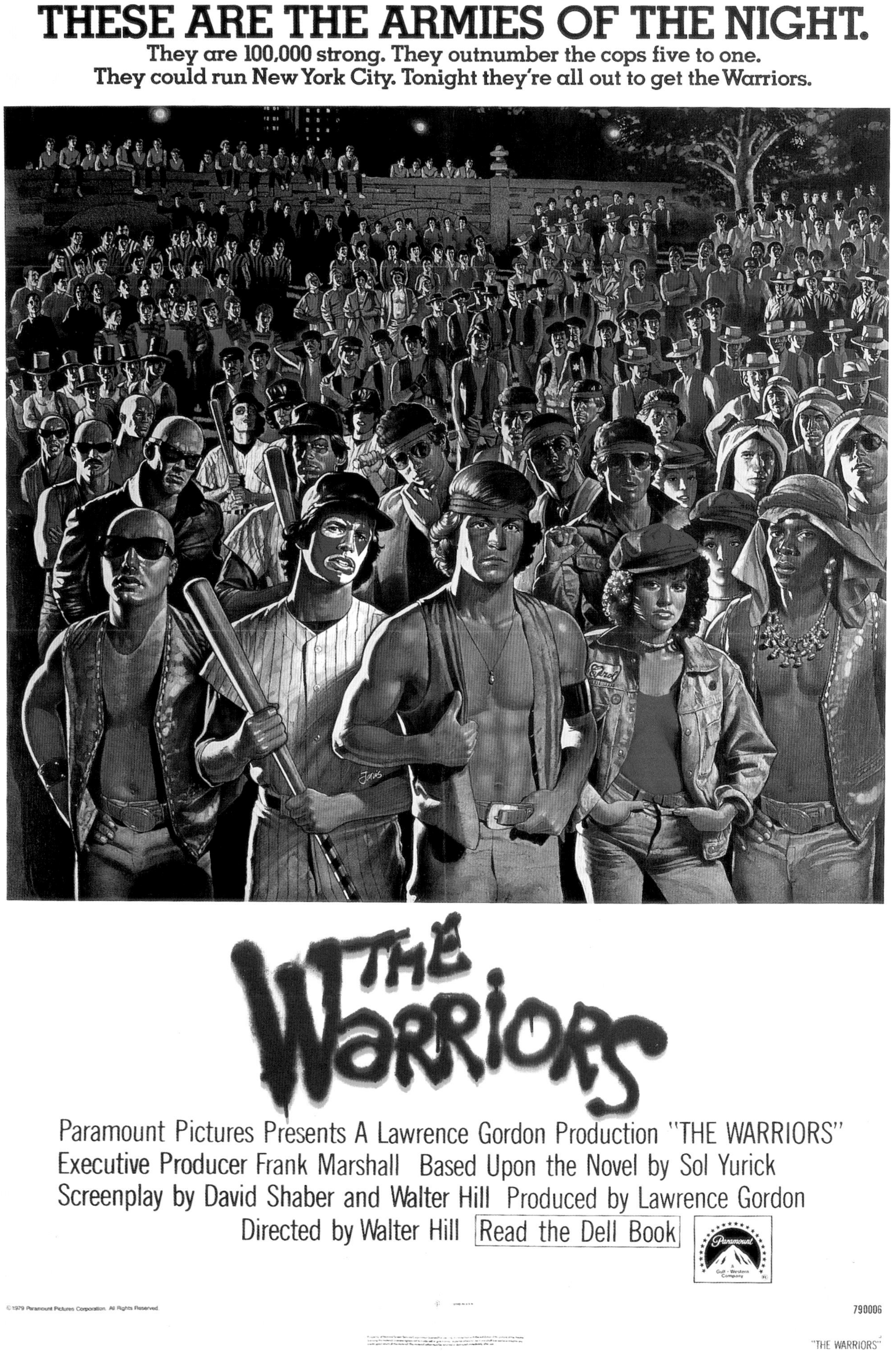

THESE ARE THE ARMIES OF THE NIGHT.
They are 100,000 strong. They outnumber the cops five to one.
They could run New York City. Tonight they're all out to get the Warriors.
THE WARRIORS
Paramount Pictures Presents A Lawrence Gordon Production "THE WARRIORS"
Executive Producer Frank Marshall Based Upon the Novel by Sol Yurick
Screenplay by David Shaber and Walter Hill Produced by Lawrence Gordon
Directed by Walter Hill
Read the Dell Book
Paramount
A Gulf + Western Company
R
©1979 Paramount Pictures Corporation. All Rights Reserved
790006
"THE WARRIORS"

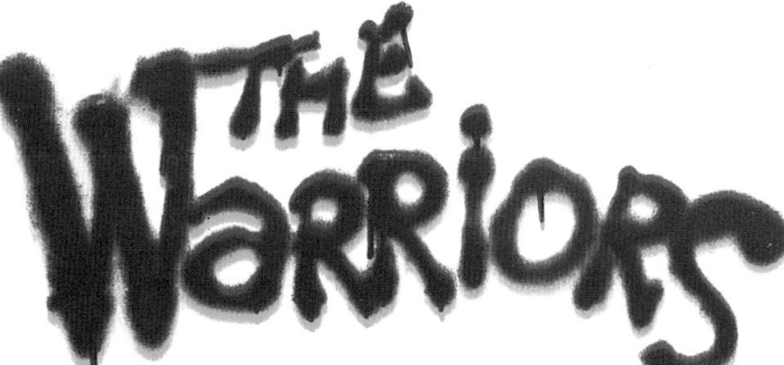

Badlands (1974)
US 41 × 27 in. (104 × 69 cm)

Starring Richard Gere Brooke Adams
Sam Shepard Linda Manz
Executive Producer Jacob Brackman
Produced by Bert and Harold Schneider
Written and Directed by Terrence Malick
A Paramount Picture
In 70MM and Dolby Six-Track Stereo Panavision®

PG PARENTAL GUIDANCE SUGGESTED

Days Of Heaven (1978)
US 36 × 14 in. (91 × 36 cm)

He was 25 years old ▪ He combed his hair like James Dean ▪ He was very fastidious ▪ People who littered bothered him ▪ She was 15 ▪ She took music lessons and could twirl a baton ▪ She wasn't very popular at school ▪ For awhile they lived together in a tree house.

In 1959, she watched while he killed a lot of people.

Badlands

PRESSMAN–WILLIAMS Presents A JILL JAKES PRODUCTION "BADLANDS"
Starring MARTIN SHEEN · SISSY SPACEK
RAMON BIERI and WARREN OATES · Executive Producer EDWARD PRESSMAN
Written, Produced and Directed by TERRENCE MALICK · From Warner Bros A Warner Communications Company PG PARENTAL GUIDANCE SUGGESTED

74/94

American Graffiti (1973)
US 41 × 27 in. (104 × 69 cm)

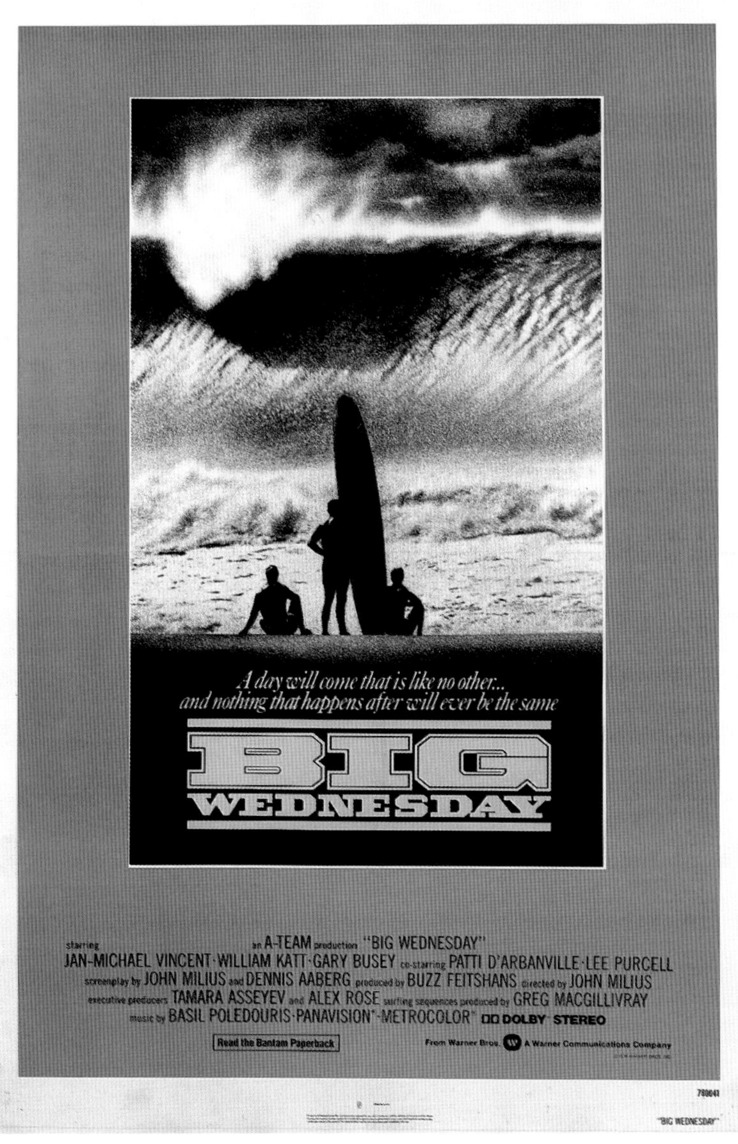

Big Wednesday (1978)
US 41 × 27 in. (104 × 69 cm)

The Last Picture Show (1971)
US 41 × 27 in. (104 × 69 cm)

When in Southern California visit UNIVERSAL STUDIOS TOUR
AN MCA COMPANY
American Graffiti
Where were you in '62?
Mels drive-in
CRUISIN'
EAT
NOW SHOWING
NO LEFT TURN
BUS STOP
"AMERICAN GRAFFITI" • A LUCASFILM LTD./COPPOLA CO. Production • Starring RICHARD DREYFUSS • RONNY HOWARD
PAUL LE MAT • CHARLIE MARTIN SMITH • CANDY CLARK • MACKENZIE PHILLIPS • CINDY WILLIAMS • WOLFMAN JACK
Written by GEORGE LUCAS and GLORIA KATZ & WILLARD HUYCK • Directed by GEORGE LUCAS
Co-Produced by GARY KURTZ • Produced by FRANCIS FORD COPPOLA • A UNIVERSAL PICTURE • TECHNICOLOR®
Original Soundtrack Album & Tapes available exclusively on MCA Records
PG PARENTAL GUIDANCE SUGGESTED
SOME MATERIAL MAY NOT BE SUITABLE FOR PRE-TEENAGERS

MIKE KAPLAN AND BUZZY ENTERPRISES PRESENT
A BIGGER
FEATURIN

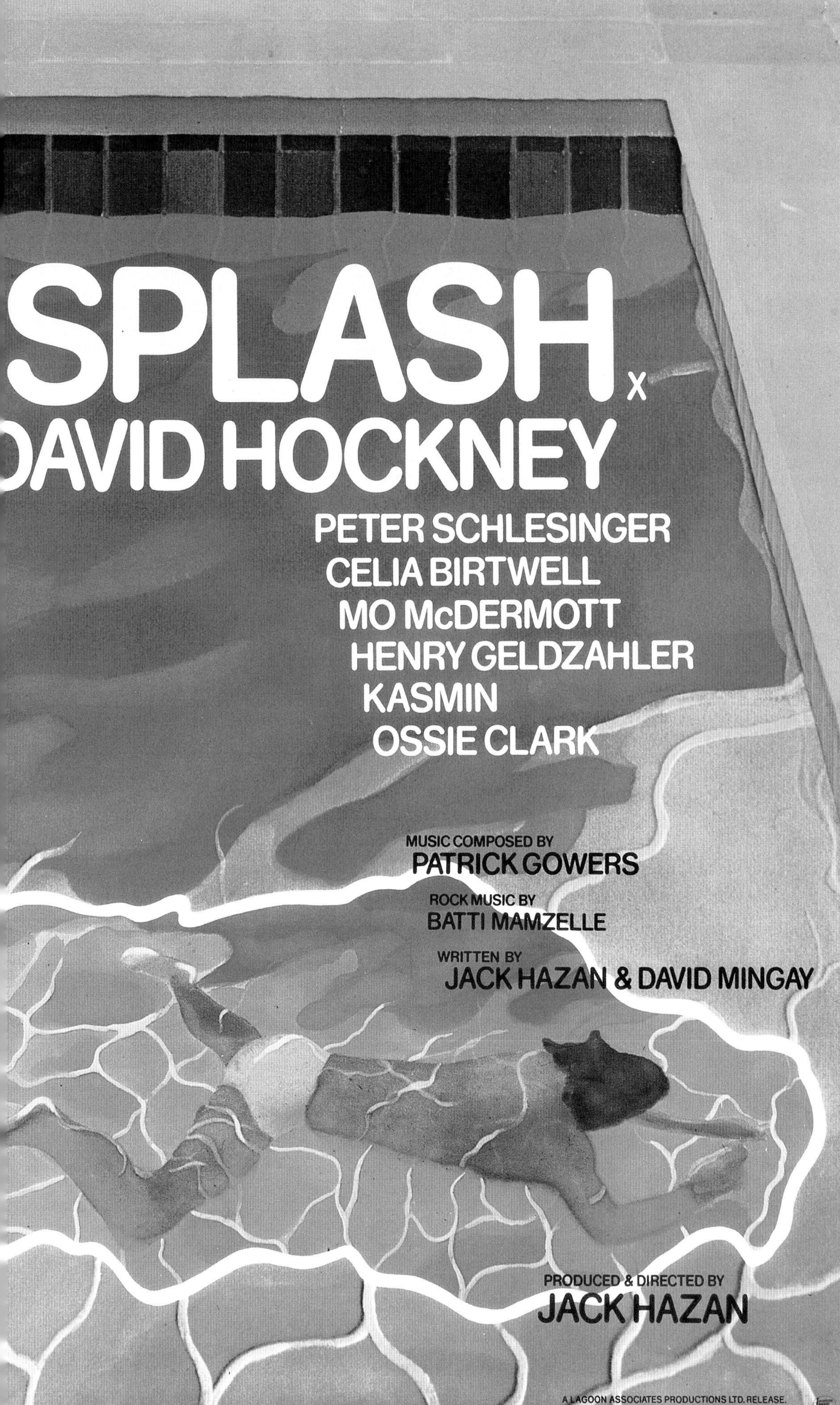

A Bigger Splash (1974)
British 30 × 40 in. (76 × 102 cm)
Featuring art by David Hockney

Jaws (1975)
US 41 x 27 in. (104 x 69 cm)

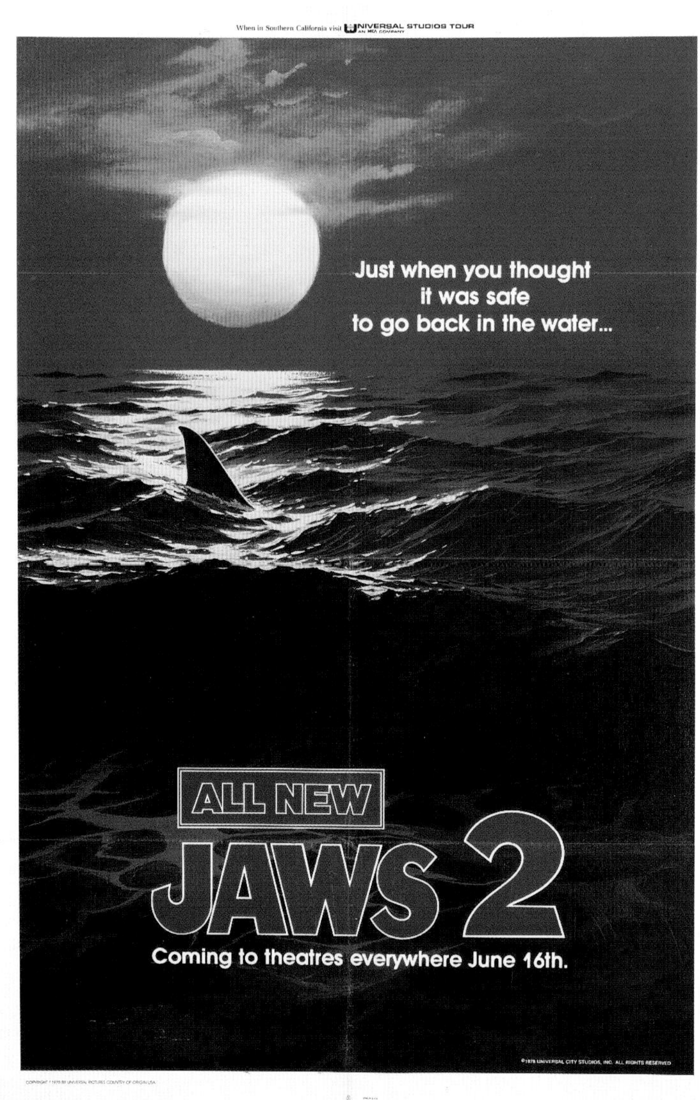

Jaws 2 (1978)
US 41 x 27 in. (104 x 69 cm)
(Advance Style B)

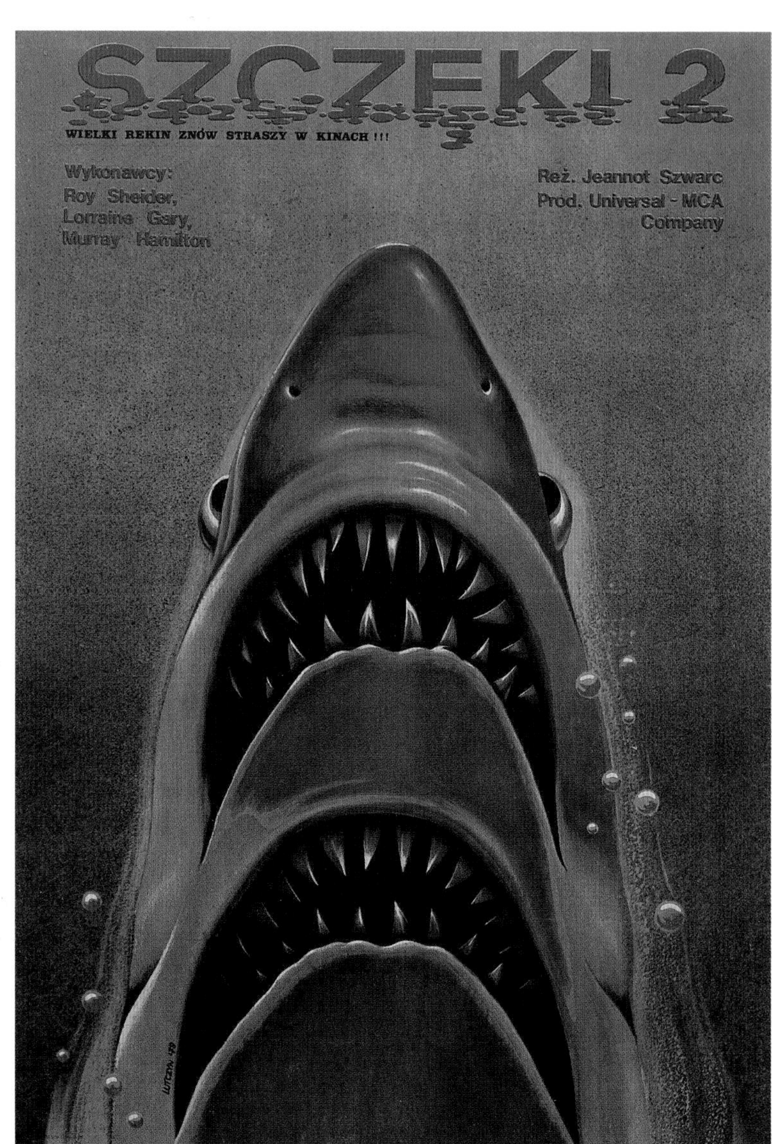

Jaws 2 / Szczeki 2 (1975)
Polish 38 x 27 in. (97 x 69 cm)

The terrifying motion picture
from the terrifying No.1 best seller.

JAWS

ROBERT SHAW
ROY SCHEIDER
RICHARD DREYFUSS

JAWS

Co-starring LORRAINE GARY · MURRAY HAMILTON · A ZANUCK/BROWN PRODUCTION

Screenplay by PETER BENCHLEY and CARL GOTTLIEB · Based on the novel by PETER BENCHLEY · Music by JOHN WILLIAMS

Directed by STEVEN SPIELBERG · Produced by RICHARD D. ZANUCK and DAVID BROWN · A UNIVERSAL PICTURE ·

TECHNICOLOR® PANAVISION®

PG PARENTAL GUIDANCE SUGGESTED
SOME MATERIAL MAY NOT BE SUITABLE FOR PRE-TEENAGERS

ORIGINAL SOUNDTRACK AVAILABLE ON MCA RECORDS & TAPES

...MAY BE TOO INTENSE FOR YOUNGER CHILDREN

75/155

"JAWS"

The Poseidon Adventure (1972)
US 41 × 27 in. (104 × 69 cm)
Art by Mort Kunstler

The Towering Inferno (1974)
US 41 × 27 in. (104 × 69 cm)

Earthquake (1974)
US 41 × 27 in. (104 × 69 cm)

At midnight on New Year's Eve the S.S. Poseidon
was struck by a 90 foot tidal wave and capsized

GENE HACKMAN · ERNEST BORGNINE · RED BUTTONS · CAROL LYNLEY · RODDY McDOWALL · STELLA STEVENS · SHELLEY WINTERS · JACK ALBERTSON · PAMELA SUE MARTIN · ARTHUR O'CONNELL · ERIC SHEA · LESLIE NIELSEN

WHO WILL SURVIVE–IN ONE OF THE GREATEST ESCAPE ADVENTURES EVER!

IRWIN ALLEN'S production of

Combining the Talents of 15 Academy Award Winners

20th Century-Fox presents "THE POSEIDON ADVENTURE" starring GENE HACKMAN · ERNEST BORGNINE · RED BUTTONS · CAROL LYNLEY · RODDY McDOWALL · STELLA STEVENS
SHELLEY WINTERS · co-starring JACK ALBERTSON · PAMELA SUE MARTIN · ARTHUR O'CONNELL · ERIC SHEA and LESLIE NIELSEN as The Captain · a RONALD NEAME film · produced by IRWIN ALLEN
directed by RONALD NEAME · screenplay by STIRLING SILLIPHANT and WENDELL MAYES · from the novel by PAUL GALLICO · music by JOHN WILLIAMS · PANAVISION® · COLOR BY DELUXE® PG

72/329

The Man With The Golden Gun (1974)
US 41 × 27 in. (104 × 69 cm)
(Advance)

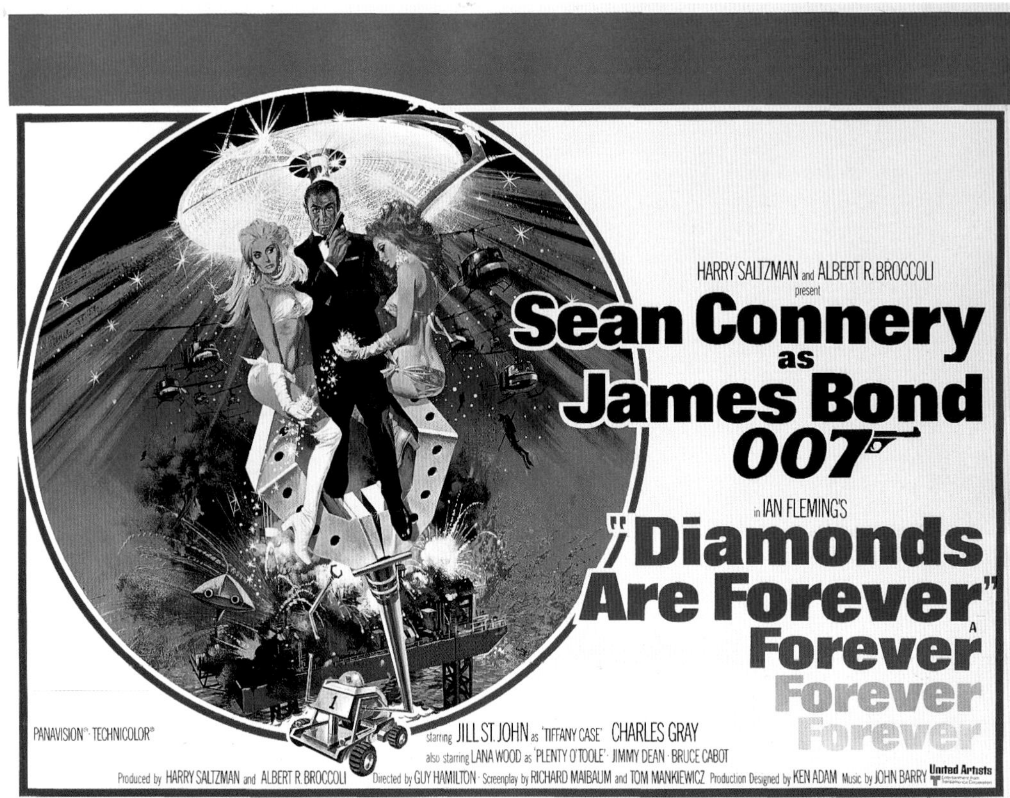

Diamonds Are Forever (1971)
British 30 × 40 in. (76 × 102 cm)
Art by Robert McGinnis

Live And Let Die (1973)
British 30 × 40 in. (76 × 102 cm)
Art by Robert McGinnis

74/251

"THE MAN WITH THE GOLDEN GUN"

Enter The Dragon (1973)
US 41 × 27 in. (104 × 69 cm)

The Bog Boss (1971)
Hong Kong 31 × 21 in. (79 × 53 cm)

Enter The Dragon (1973)
Hong Kong 31 × 21 in. (79 × 53 cm)

Their deadly mission: to crack the forbidden island of Han!

POLICE
Enter The Dragon
The ultimate Martial Arts masterpiece! Lavishly filmed by Warner Bros. in Hong Kong and the China Sea!

CO-STARRING

BRUCE LEE · JOHN SAXON · AHNA CAPRI in **"ENTER THE DRAGON" BOB WALL · SHIH KIEN** and Introducing **JIM KELLY**

Music: Lalo Schifrin · Written by Michael Allin · Produced by Fred Weintraub and Paul Heller in association with Raymond Chow · Directed by Robert Clouse

R RESTRICTED Under 17 requires accompanying Parent or Adult Guardian — PANAVISION® · TECHNICOLOR® · Celebrating Warner Bros. 50th Anniversary — A Warner Communications Company

ORIGINAL SOUND TRACK ALBUM ON WARNER BROS. RECORDS

73/268

"ENTER THE DRAGON"

The Yakuza (1975)
US International
41 x 27 in. (104 x 69 cm)
Art by Bob Peak

The Spy Who Loved Me (1977)
US 41 x 27 in. (104 x 69 cm)
Art by Bob Peak

Rollerball (1975)
US 41 x 27 in. (104 x 69 cm)
Art by Bob Peak

Superman (1978)
US 41 x 27 in. (104 x 69 cm)
Art by Bob Peak

Star Trek – The Motion Picture (1979)
US 41 x 27 in. (104 x 69 cm)
Art by Bob Peak

Apocalypse Now (1979)
US 41 x 27 in. (104 x 69 cm)
Art by Bob Peak

75/20

"ROLLERBALL"

A Woman Under The Influence (1974)
US 41 x 27 in. (104 x 69 cm)
(Style E)
Art Director & Photographer: Sam Shaw

A Woman Under The Influence (1974)
US 41 x 27 in. (104 x 69 cm)
(Style D)
Art Director & Photographer: Sam Shaw

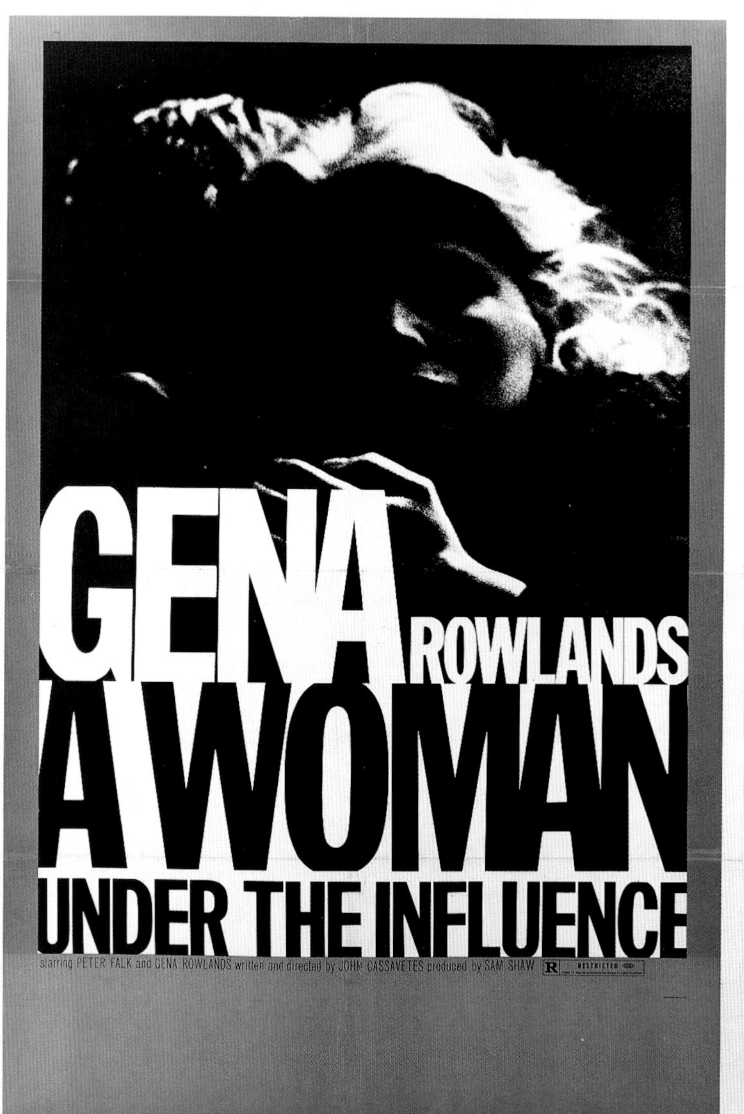

A Woman Under The Influence (1974)
US 41 x 27 in. (104 x 69 cm)
(Style A)
Art Director & Photographer: Sam Shaw

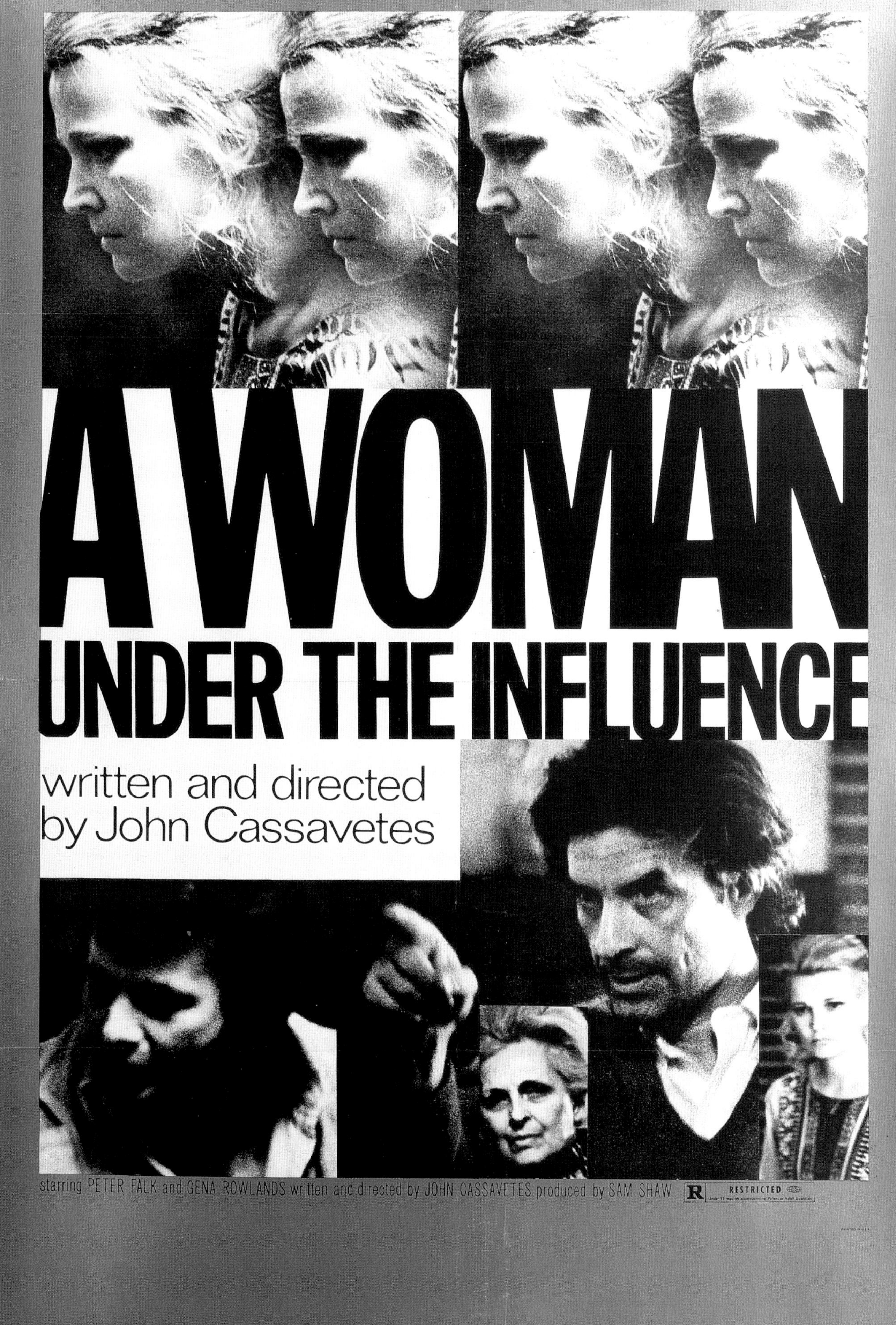
A WOMAN
UNDER THE INFLUENCE
written and directed
by John Cassavetes
starring PETER FALK and GENA ROWLANDS written and directed by JOHN CASSAVETES produced by SAM SHAW
R
RESTRICTED

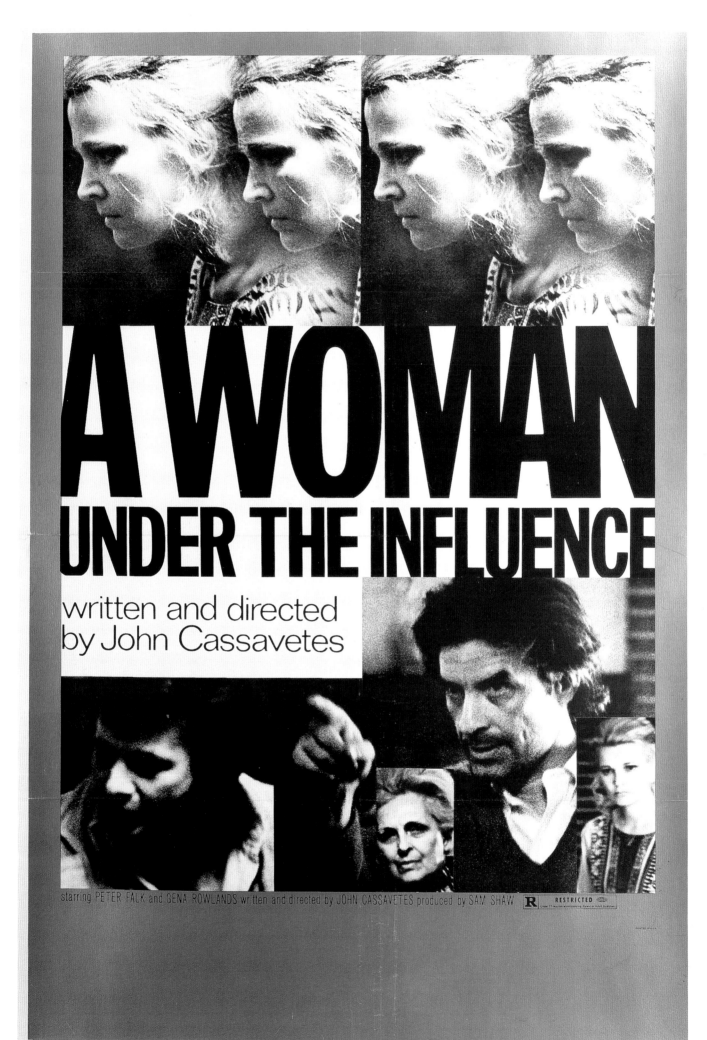

Husbands (1970)
US 41 × 27 in. (104 × 69 cm)

The Killing Of A Chinese Bookie (1976)
US 41 × 27 in. (104 × 69 cm)
(Style A)
Photograph by Sam Shaw

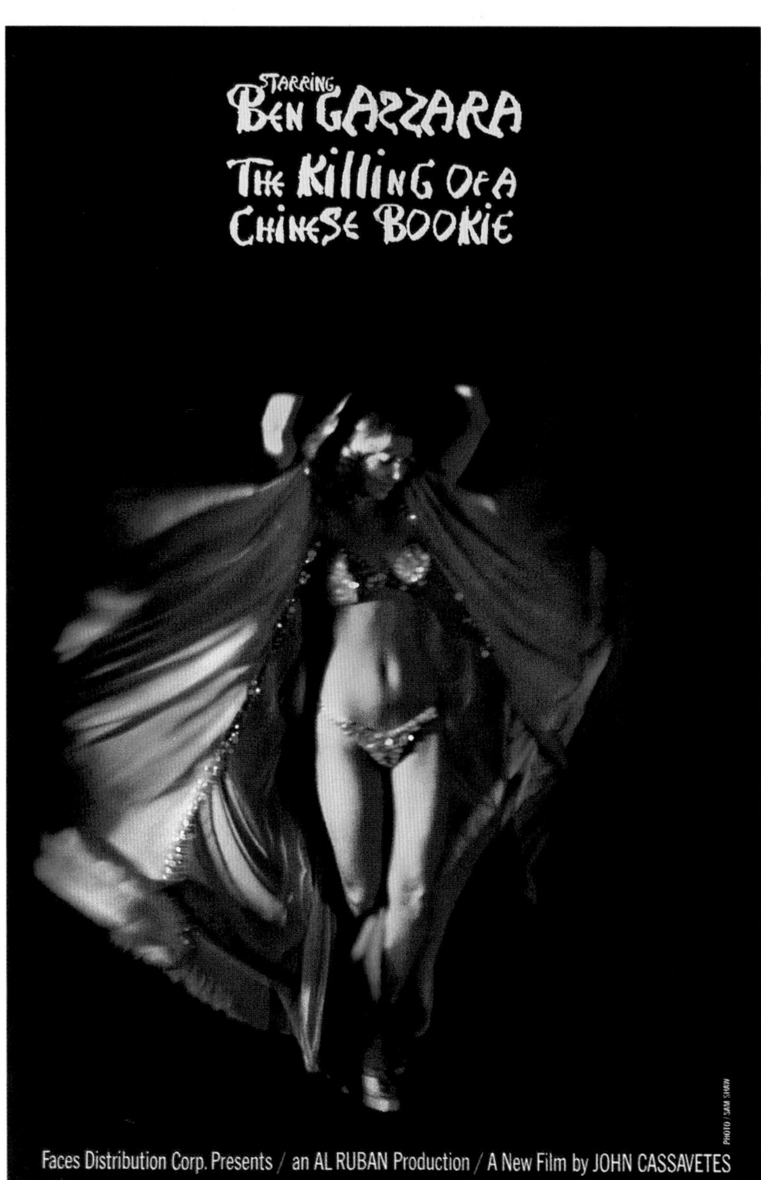

The Killing Of A Chinese Bookie (1976)
US 41 × 27 in. (104 × 69 cm)
(Style B)
Photograph by Sam Shaw

A comedy
about life,
death
and freedom

AL RUBAN
and
SAM SHAW
Present

BEN
GAZZARA
PETER
FALK
JOHN
CASSAVETES
in
HUSBANDS

Produced by AL RUBAN Associate Producer SAM SHAW Written and Directed by JOHN CASSAVETES
FROM COLUMBIA PICTURES GP ALL AGES ADMITTED

70/221

Il Conformista / Le Conformiste (1970)
French 63 × 47 in. (160 × 119 cm)
Art by Piero Ermanno Iaia

1900 (1977)
US 41 × 27 in. (104 × 69 cm)
Art by Doug Johnson

CINEMA INTERNATIONAL CORPORATION présente UNE PRODUCTION MARS FILM
JEAN-LOUIS TRINTIGNANT
STEFANIA SANDRELLI
dans
LE CONFORMISTE
ERMANNO IAIA
avec
GASTONE MOSCHIN · ENZO TARASCIO
FOSCO GIACHETTI · JOSE QUAGLIO
avec DOMINIQUE SANDA dans le rôle de ANNA
et la participation de
PIERRE CLEMENTI
Producteur associé GIOVANNI BERTOLUCCI
Produit par MAURIZIO LODI-FE
Réalisé par BERNARDO BERTOLUCCI
D'après le roman de ALBERTO MORAVIA
TECHNICOLOR
Musique composée et dirigée par GEORGES DELERUE
Une coproduction MARS FILM PRODUZIONE S.p.A. ROME · MARIANNE PRODUCTIONS PARIS
Distribuée par CINEMA INTERNATIONAL CORPORATION
LALANDE-COURBET 91-WISSOUS
Visa de Contrôle n° 4071

Aguirre Der Zorn Gottes
(Aguirre, Wrath Of God) (1972)
German 33 × 23 in. (84 × 58 cm)

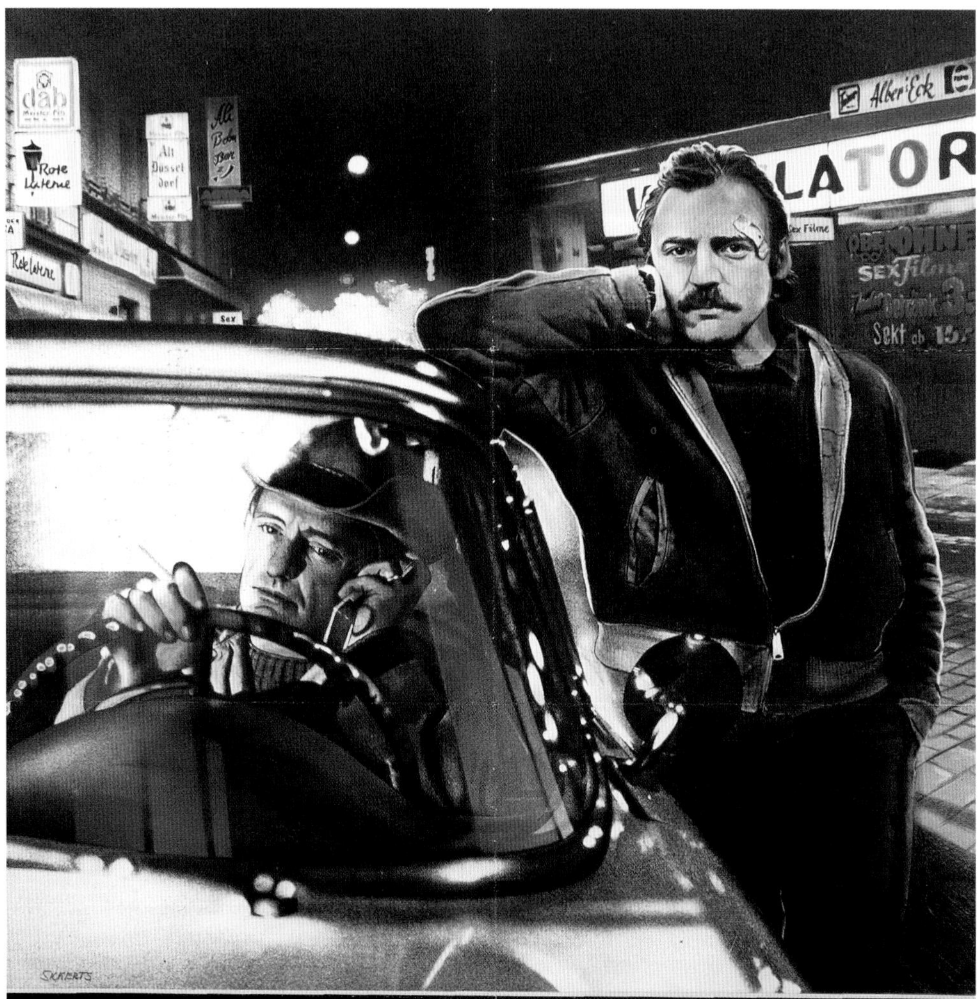

Der Amerikanische Freund
(The American Friend) (1977)
German 33 × 23 in. (84 × 58 cm)
Art by Sickerts

KLAUS
KINSKI
als
AGUIRRE
DER ZORN
GOTTES
Ein Film von
Werner Herzog
mit
Helena Rojo
Del Negro
Ruy Guerra
Peter Berling
Cecilia Rivera
Dany Ades
Armando Polanah
Kamera:
Thomas Mauch
Musik:
Popol Vuh
Werner Herzog
Filmproduktion
Verleih:
Filmverlag
der Autoren
Weltvertrieb:
Cine-International

Murder On The Orient Express (1974)
US 41 × 27 in. (104 × 69 cm)
Art by Richard Amsel

The Sting (1974)
US 41 × 27 in. (104 × 69 cm)
Art by Richard Amsel
Art Director: Bill Gold

The Life And Times Of Judge Roy Bean (1972)
US 41 × 27 in. (104 × 69 cm)
Art by Richard Amsel

The Shootist (1976)
US 41 × 27 in. (104 × 69 cm)
Art by Richard Amsel

McCabe And Mrs. Miller (1971)
US 41 × 27 in. (104 × 69 cm)
Art by Richard Amsel

Sweet Sweetback's Baadasssss Song (1971)
US 41 × 27 in. (104 × 69 cm)

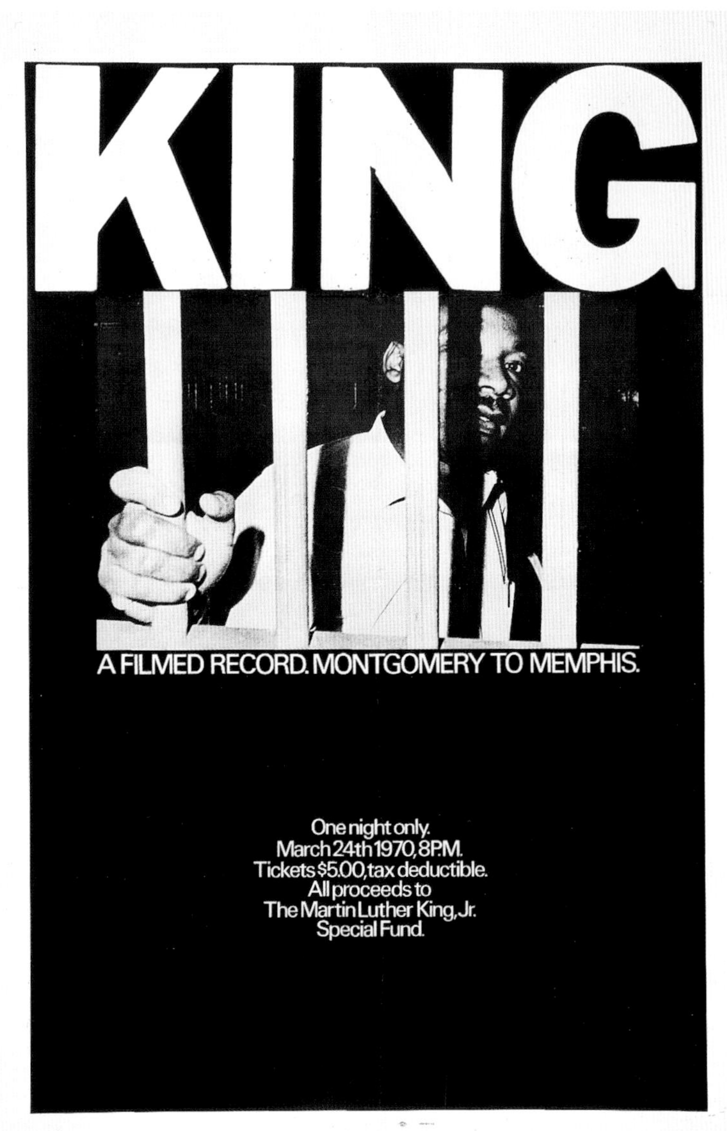

**King: A Filmed Record....
Montgomery To Memphis** (1970)
US 41 × 27 in. (104 × 69 cm)

A.K.A. Cassius Clay (1970)
US International
41 × 27 in. (104 × 69 cm)

SWEET SWEETBACK

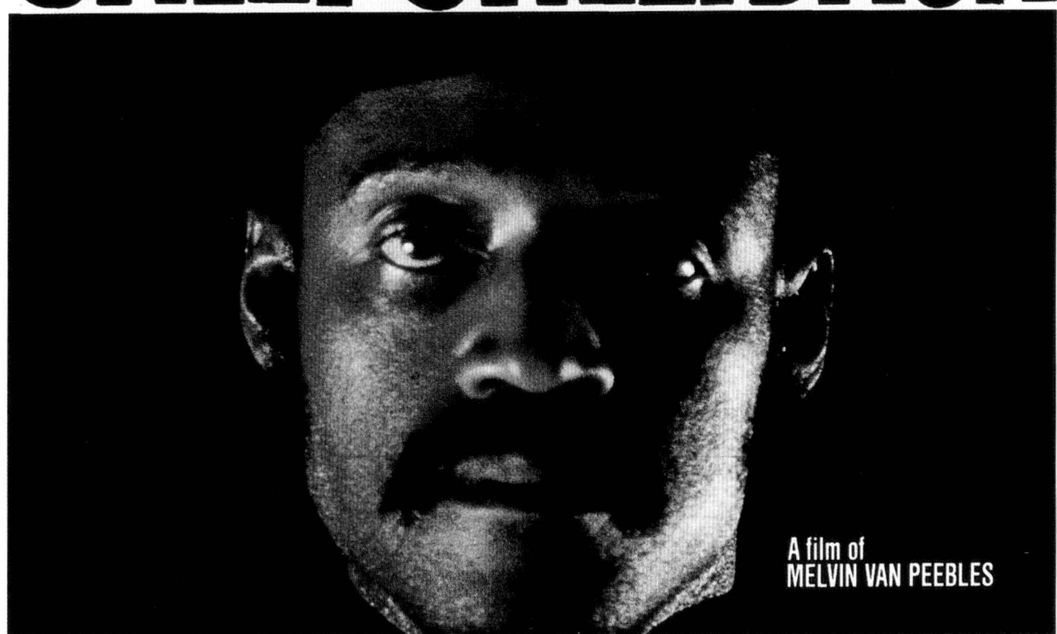

YOU BLED MY MOMMA — YOU BLED MY POPPA — BUT YOU WONT BLEED ME

ORIGINAL SOUNDTRACK ALBUM AVAILABLE ON STAX RECORDS
ORIGINAL PAPERBACK SOON AVAILABLE AS A LANCER PUBLICATION
MELVIN VAN PEEBLES and JERRY GROSS present "SWEET SWEETBACK'S BAADASSSSS SONG"
a CINEMATION INDUSTRIES Release • COLOR

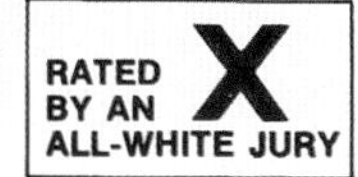

Never a dude like this one!
He's got a plan to stick it to The Man!

Superfly (1972)
US 41 × 27 in. (104 × 69 cm)

Foxy Brown (1974)
US 41 × 27 in. (104 × 69 cm)

ONE CAT...
WHO PLAYS LIKE AN ARMY!

HIS FRIENDS CALL HIM MR. T...HIS ENEMIES CALL FOR MERCY!

20TH CENTURY-FOX Presents TROUBLE MAN Starring ROBERT HOOKS
Co-Starring PAUL WINFIELD RALPH WAITE BILL SMITHERS PAULA KELLY JULIUS HARRIS
Produced by JOEL D. FREEMAN · Executive Producer JOHN D. F. BLACK · Directed by IVAN DIXON
Written by JOHN D. F. BLACK Music by MARVIN GAYE
COLOR BY DE LUXE

Original MARVIN GAYE SCORE
Available On MOTOWN RECORDS
TWENTIETH CENTURY-FOX

Trouble Man (1972)
US 41 × 27 in. (104 × 69 cm)

Shaft (1971)
US 41 × 27 in. (104 × 69 cm)

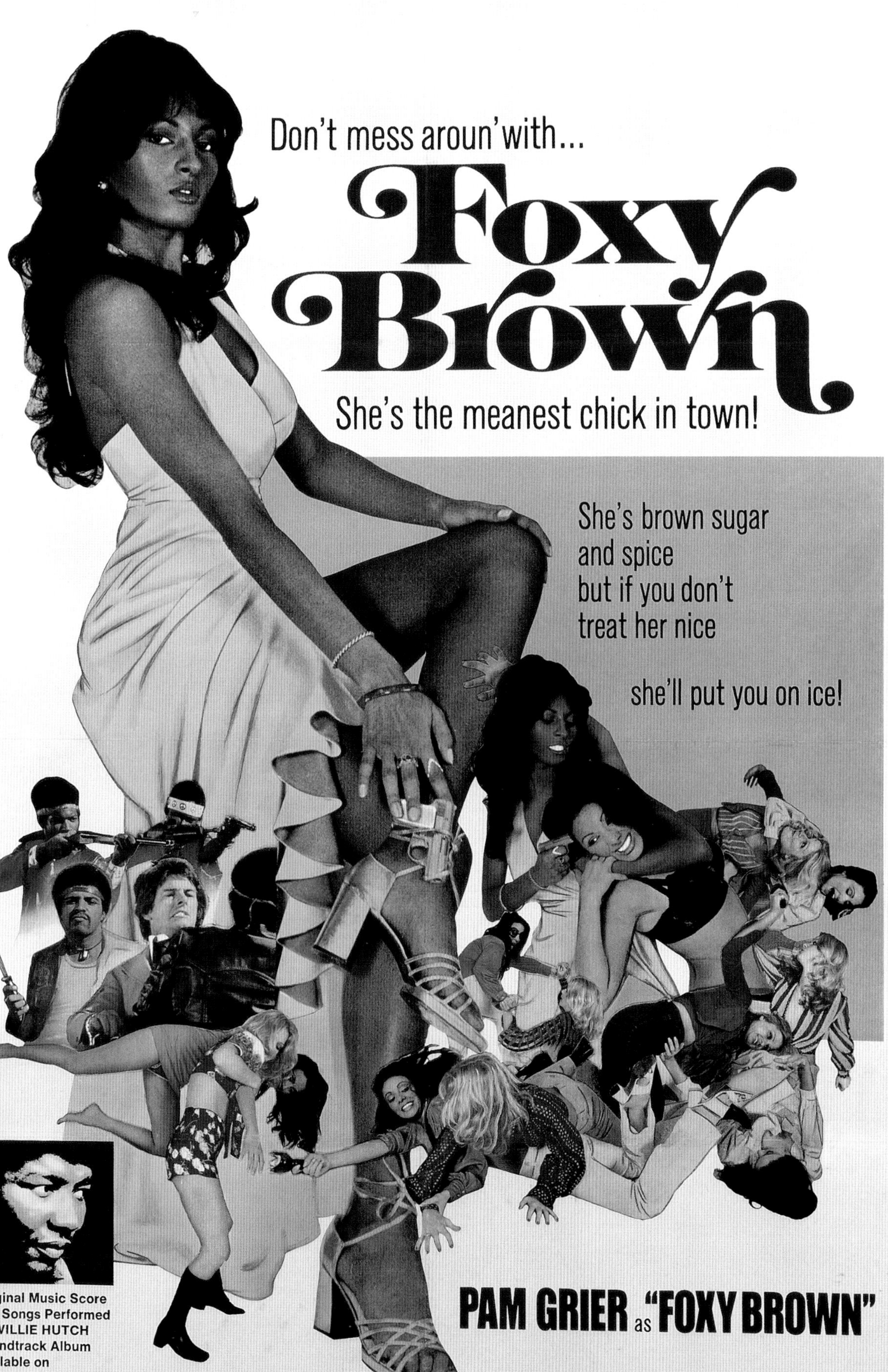
Don't mess aroun' with...
Foxy Brown
She's the meanest chick in town!
She's brown sugar
and spice
but if you don't
treat her nice
she'll put you on ice!
Original Music Score
and Songs Performed
by WILLIE HUTCH
Soundtrack Album
available on
Motown Records
PAM GRIER as "FOXY BROWN"
R RESTRICTED
Under 17 Requires Accompanying
Parent or Adult Guardian
Also starring PETER BROWN · TERRY CARTER as Michael · Co-starring KATHRYN LODER · HARRY HOLCOMBE
Produced by BUZZ FEITSHANS · Written and Directed by JACK HILL · COLOR by Movielab · An AMERICAN INTERNATIONAL Picture
COPYRIGHT ©1974 AMERICAN INTERNATIONAL PICTURES, INC.
74/100

Star Wars (1977)
Polish 38 × 27 in. (97 × 69 cm)
Art by Jakub Erol

Star Wars (1977)
US 41 × 27 in. (104 × 69 cm)
(Style C)
Art by Tom William Chantrell

Star Wars (1977)
US 41 × 27 in. (104 × 69 cm)
(Style D)
Art by Drew Struzan & Charles White III

Star Wars (1977)
US 29 × 20 in. (74 × 51 cm)
Art by Howard Chaykin

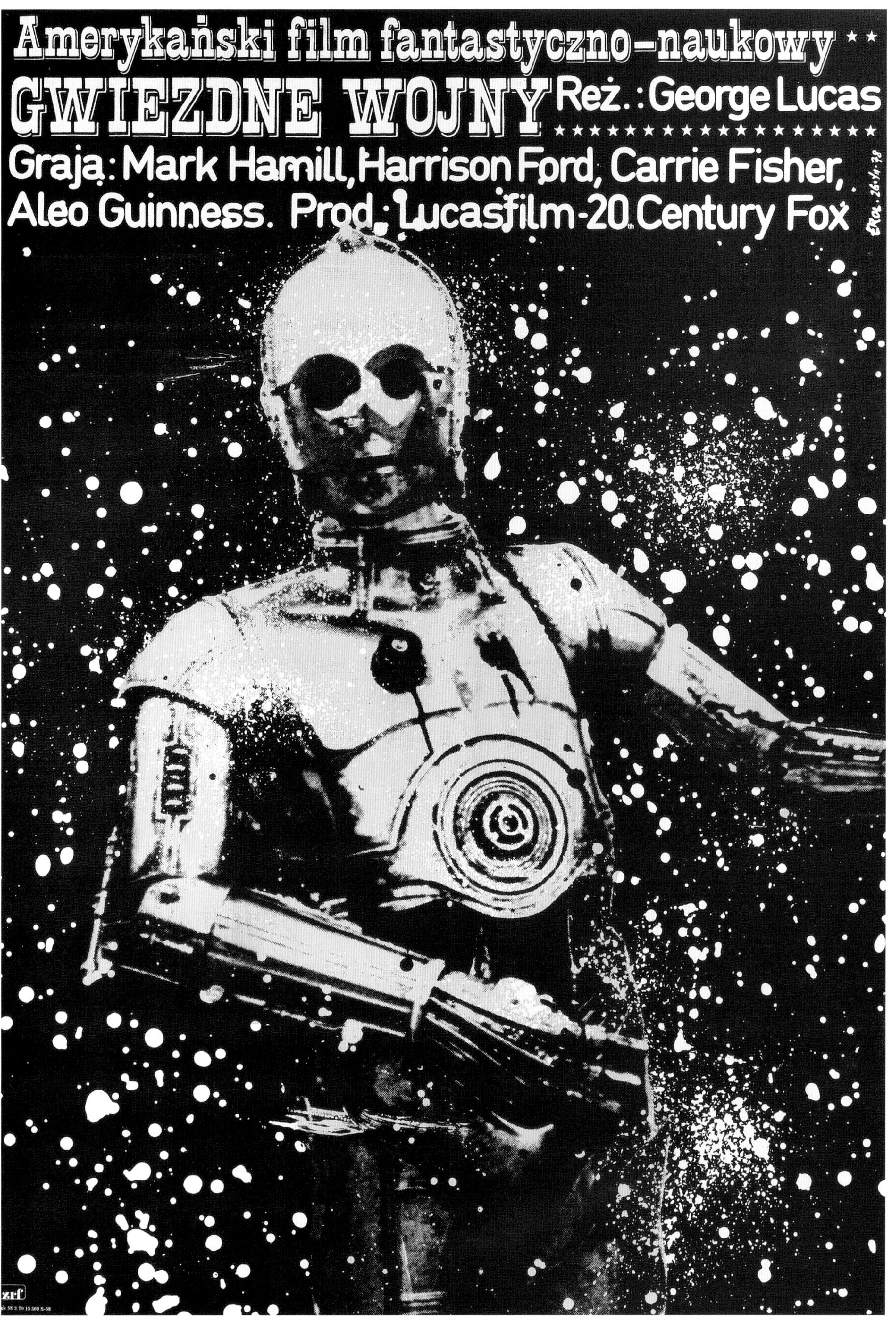
Amerykański film fantastyczno-naukowy
GWIEZDNE WOJNY Reż.: George Lucas
Grają: Mark Hamill, Harrison Ford, Carrie Fisher, Aleo Guinness. Prod.: Lucasfilm-20th Century Fox

Alien (1979)
US 41 × 27 in. (104 × 69 cm)
Design by Philip Gips

The Man Who Fell To Earth (1976)
British 30 × 40 in. (76 × 102 cm)
Art by Vic Fair

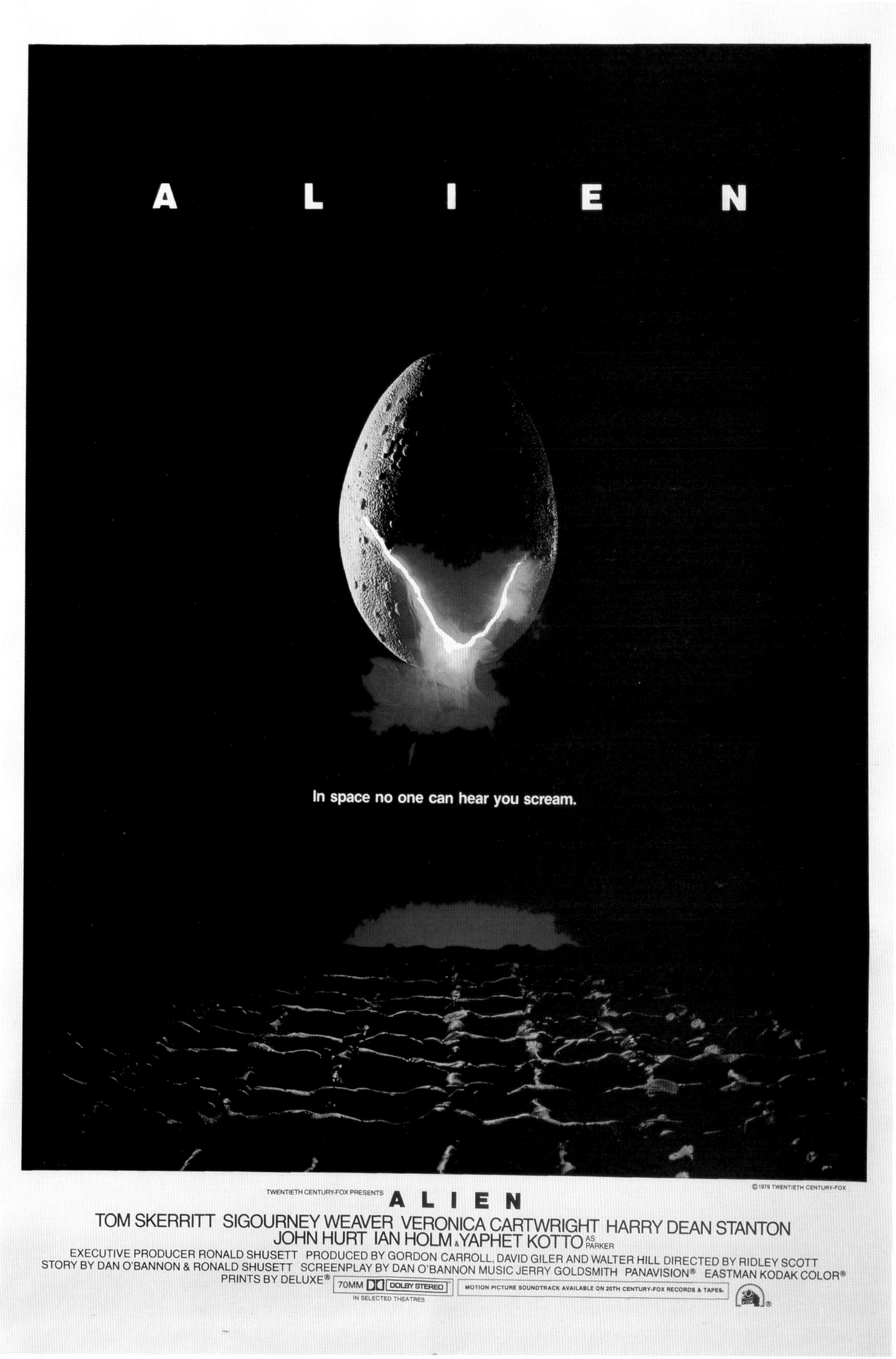

A L I E N
In space no one can hear you scream.
TWENTIETH CENTURY-FOX PRESENTS
A L I E N
©1979 TWENTIETH CENTURY-FOX
TOM SKERRITT SIGOURNEY WEAVER VERONICA CARTWRIGHT HARRY DEAN STANTON
JOHN HURT IAN HOLM & YAPHET KOTTO AS PARKER
EXECUTIVE PRODUCER RONALD SHUSETT PRODUCED BY GORDON CARROLL, DAVID GILER AND WALTER HILL DIRECTED BY RIDLEY SCOTT
STORY BY DAN O'BANNON & RONALD SHUSETT SCREENPLAY BY DAN O'BANNON MUSIC JERRY GOLDSMITH PANAVISION® EASTMAN KODAK COLOR®
PRINTS BY DELUXE®
70MM DOLBY STEREO
IN SELECTED THEATRES
MOTION PICTURE SOUNDTRACK AVAILABLE ON 20TH CENTURY-FOX RECORDS & TAPES.

THX 1138 (1970)
US 41 × 27 in. (104 × 69 cm)

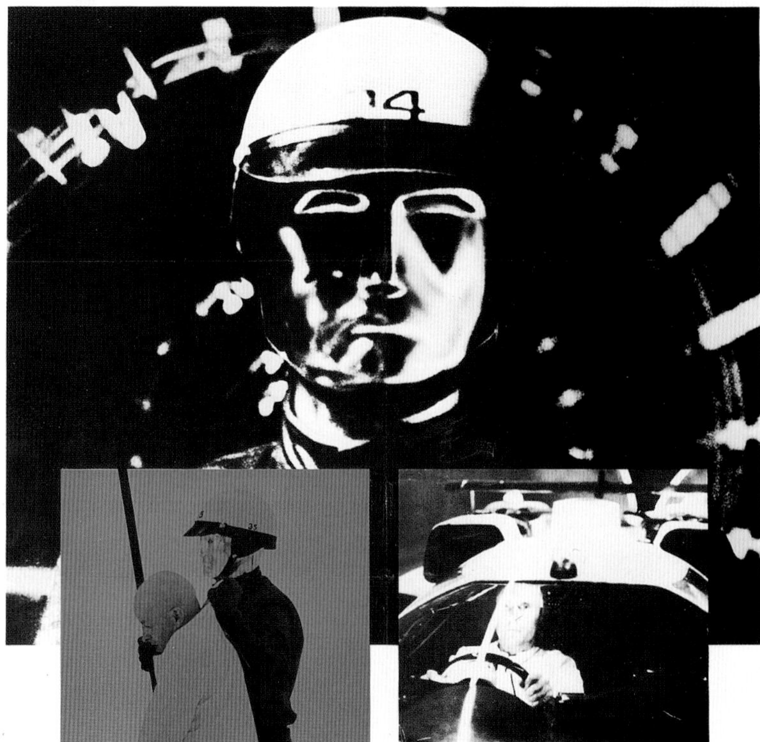

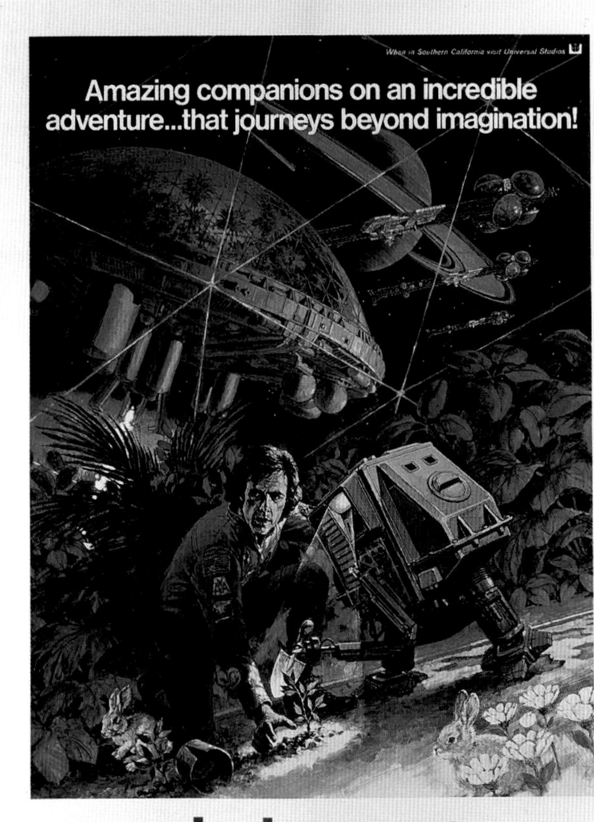

Silent Running (1971)
US 41 × 27 in. (104 × 69 cm)

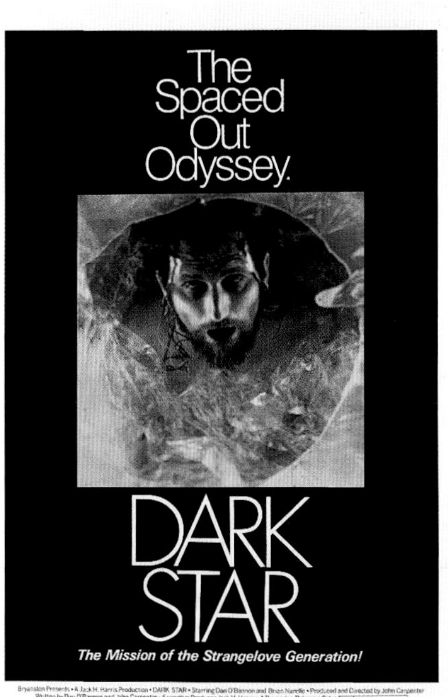

Dark Star (1974)
US 41 × 27 in. (104 × 69 cm)

Westworld (1973)
US 41 × 27 in. (104 × 69 cm)

BOY, HAVE WE GOT A VACATION FOR YOU...

WESTWORLD

...Where nothing can possibly go worng!

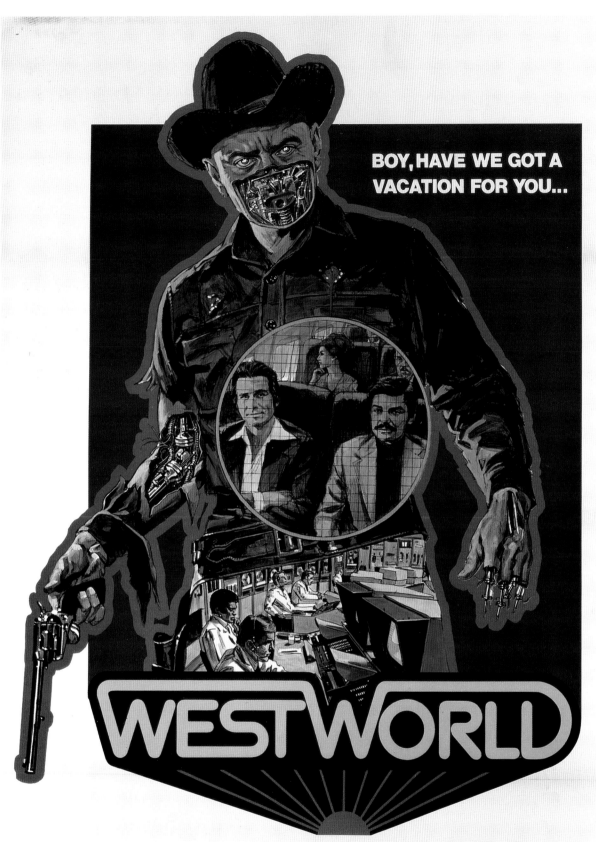

MGM Presents "WESTWORLD" Starring YUL BRYNNER RICHARD BENJAMIN JAMES BROLIN · Music FRED KARLIN · Written and Directed by MICHAEL CRICHTON · Produced by PAUL N. LAZARUS III

MGM

PG PARENTAL GUIDANCE SUGGESTED Some material may not be suitable for pre-teenagers

PANAVISION® METROCOLOR

The Outlaw Josey Wales (1976)
US 41 × 27 in. (104 × 69 cm)

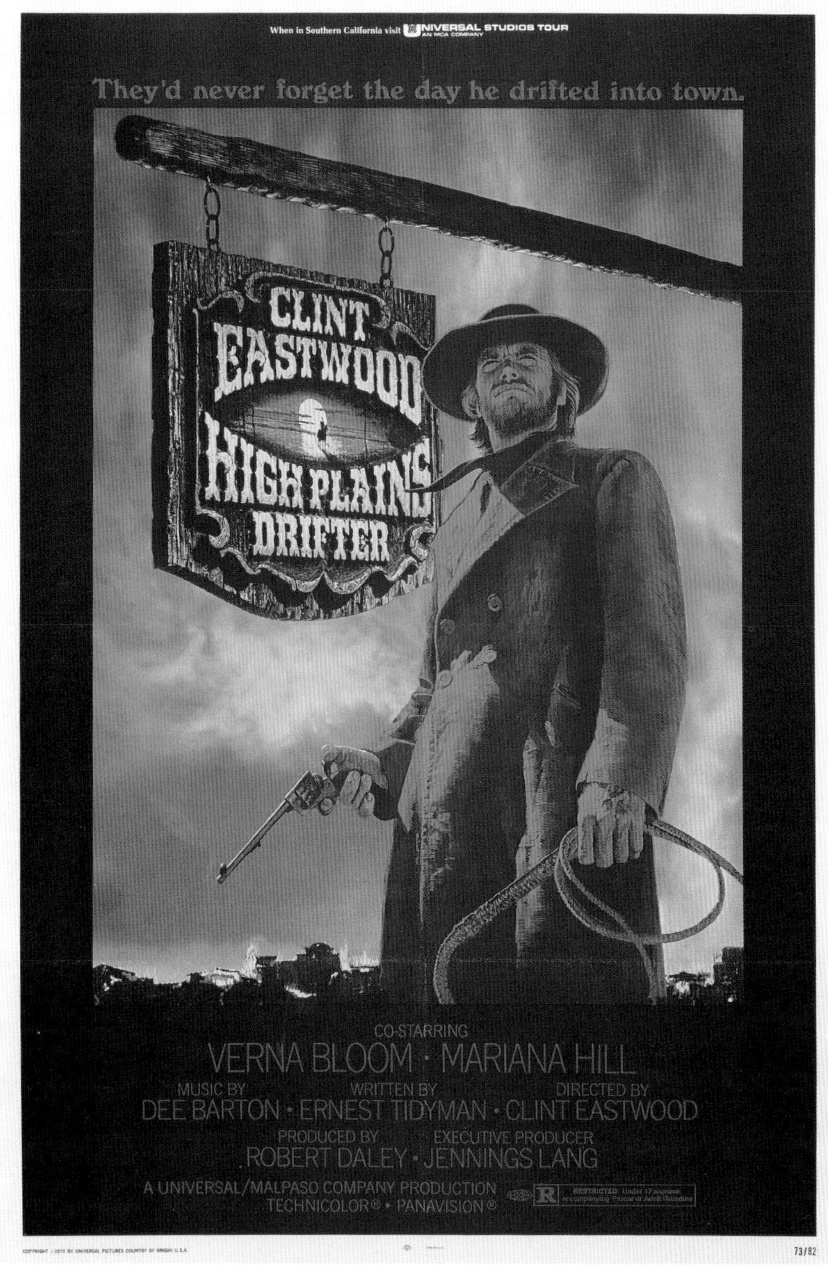

High Plains Drifter (1973)
US 41 × 27 in. (104 × 69 cm)

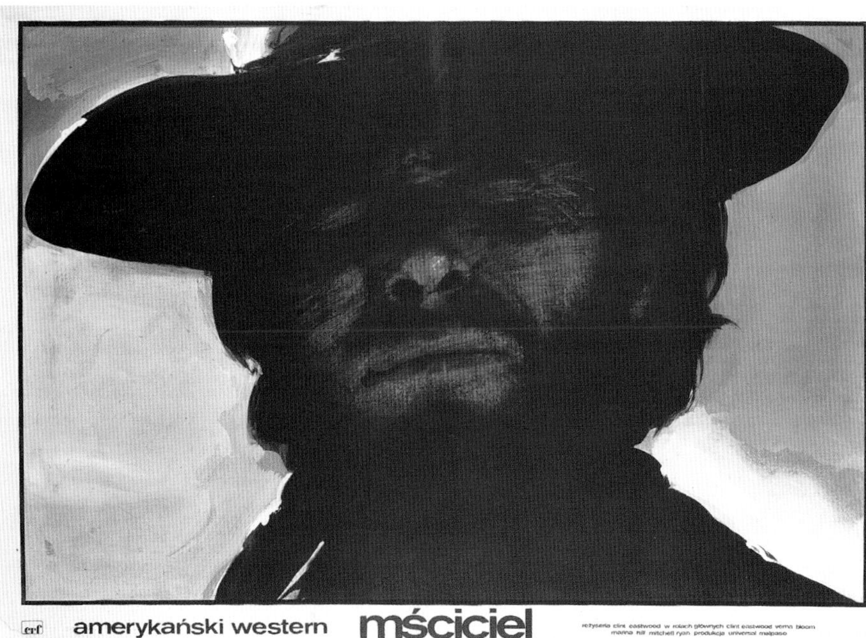

High Plains Drifter / Msciciel (1973)
Polish 23 × 32 in. (58 × 81 cm)

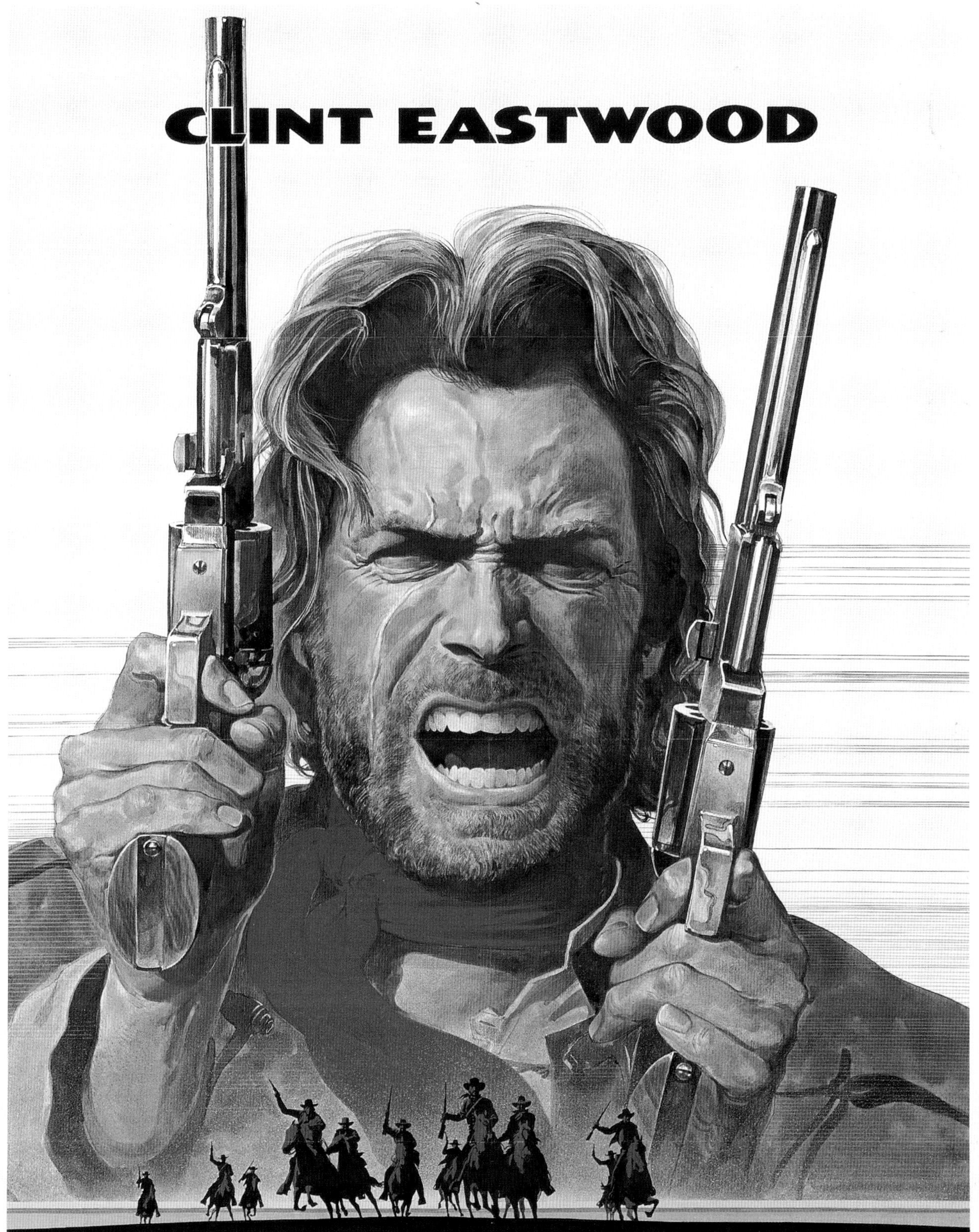
CLINT EASTWOOD
THE
OUTLAW JOSEY WALES
...an army of one.
CLINT EASTWOOD "THE OUTLAW JOSEY WALES" A MALPASO COMPANY FILM · CHIEF DAN GEORGE · SONDRA LOCKE · BILL McKINNEY
and JOHN VERNON as Fletcher · Screenplay by PHIL KAUFMAN and SONIA CHERNUS · Produced by ROBERT DALEY · Directed by CLINT EASTWOOD
Music by JERRY FIELDING · Panavision® Color by De Luxe® Distributed by Warner Bros. A Warner Communications Company
PG PARENTAL GUIDANCE SUGGESTED
COPYRIGHT © 1976 WARNER BROS., INC.
76/152

Billy Jack (1971)
US International
41 × 27 in. (104 × 69 cm)
Art by Piero Ermanno Iaia

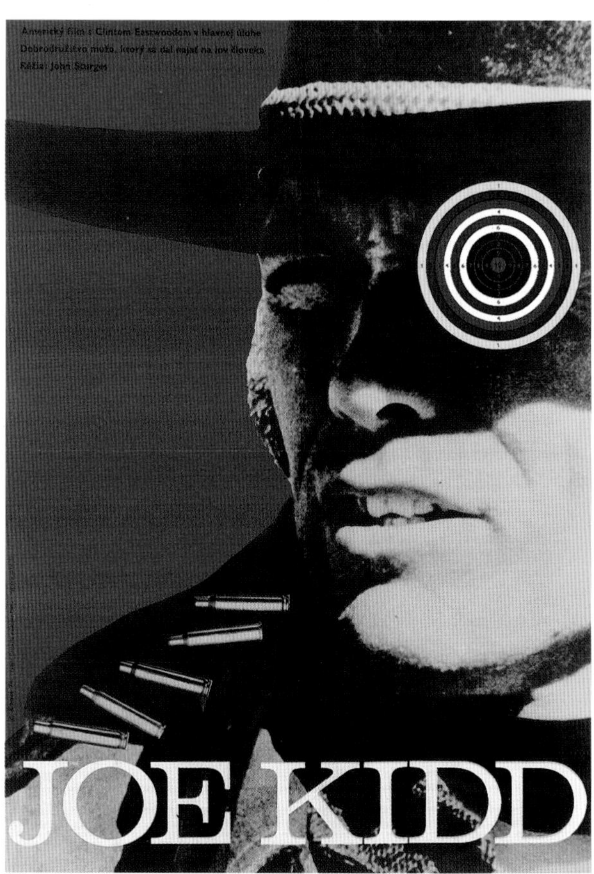

Joe Kid / Joe Kidd (1972)
Czech 33 × 23 in. (84 × 58 cm)

The Beguiled (1971)
US 41 × 27 in. (104 × 69 cm)

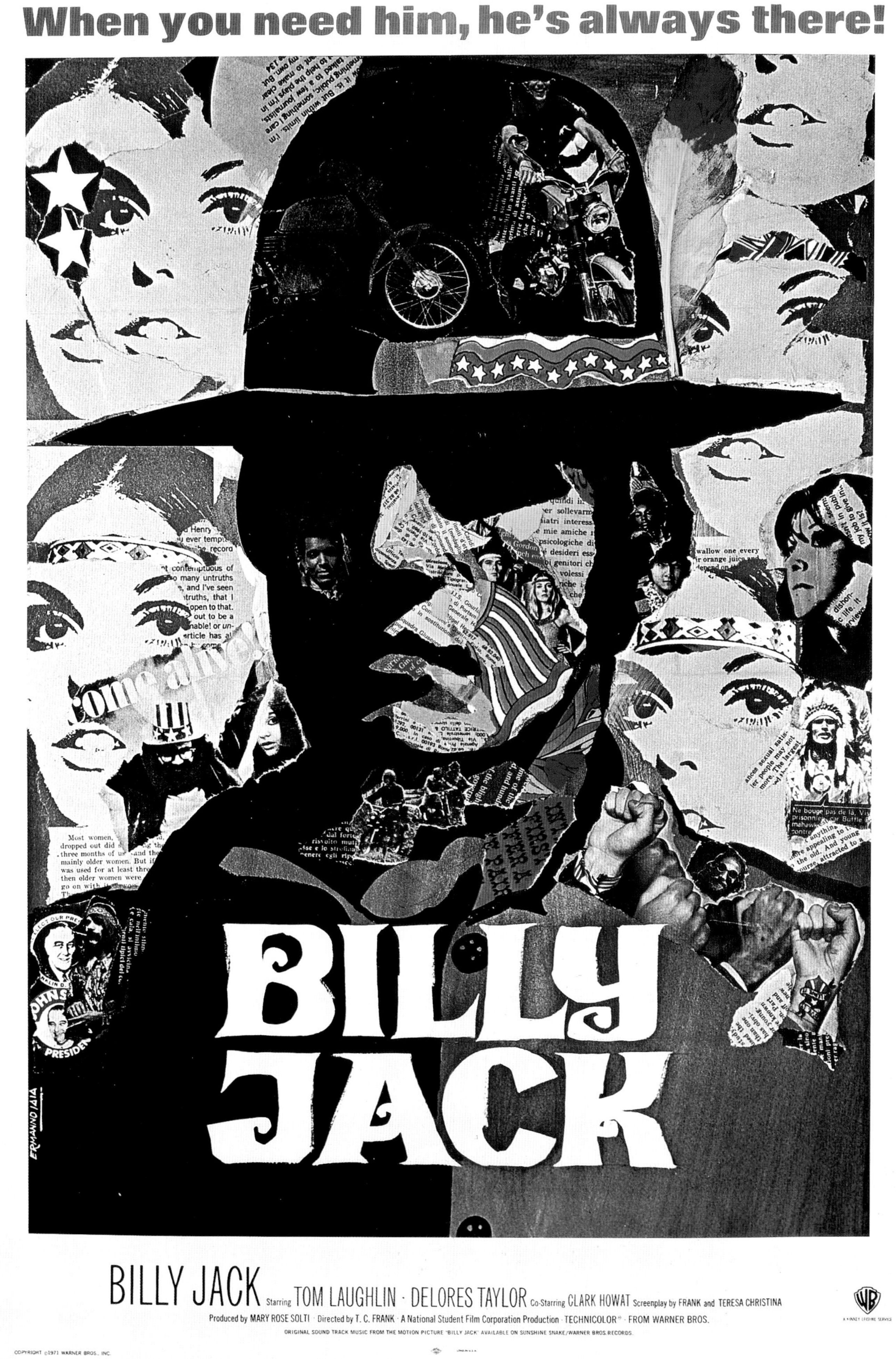

When you need him, he's always there!

BILLY JACK

BILLY JACK Starring TOM LAUGHLIN · DELORES TAYLOR Co-Starring CLARK HOWAT Screenplay by FRANK and TERESA CHRISTINA

Produced by MARY ROSE SOLTI · Directed by T. C. FRANK · A National Student Film Corporation Production · TECHNICOLOR® · FROM WARNER BROS.

ORIGINAL SOUND TRACK MUSIC FROM THE MOTION PICTURE "BILLY JACK" AVAILABLE ON SUNSHINE SNAKE/WARNER BROS. RECORDS.

Cabaret / Kabaret (1972)
Polish 33 × 23 in. (84 × 58 cm)
Art by Wiktor Gorka

Solaris (1972)
Polish 33 × 23 in. (84 × 58 cm)
Art by Bertrandt

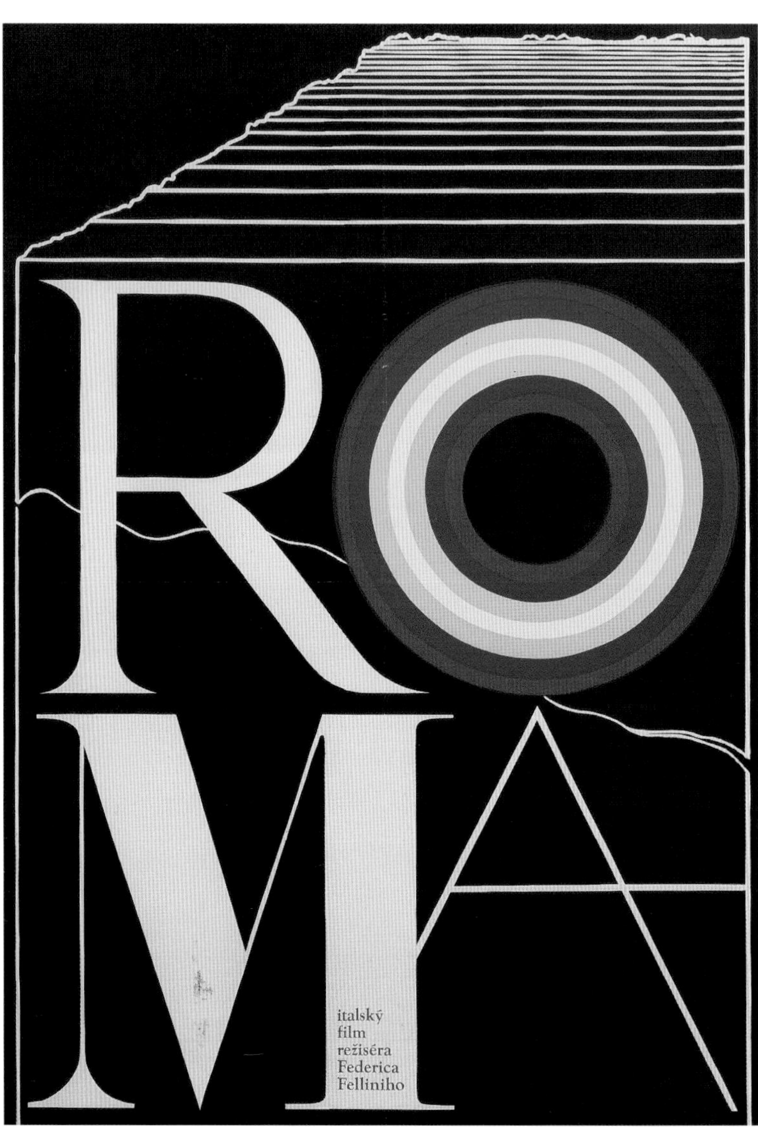

Roma (1972)
Czech 33 × 23 in. (84 × 58 cm)

KABARET
Produkcja: Feurer and Martin
Amerykański musical filmowy
nagrodzony 7 Oscarami
Reżyseria
BOB FOSSE
W głównych rolach
LIZA MINELLI
Michael York
Joel Grey
W. GÓRKA 73

Le Fantôme De La Liberté (The Phantom Of Liberty) (1974)
French 31 × 24 in. (79 × 61 cm)
Art by René Ferracci

Le Charme Discret De La Bourgeoisie (The Discreet Charm Of The Bourgeoisie) (1972)
French 31 × 24 in. (79 × 61 cm)
Art by René Ferracci

SERGE SILBERMAN présente

le charme discret de la bourgeoisie

avec par ordre
d'entrée en scène
FERNANDO REY
PAUL FRANKEUR
DELPHINE SEYRIG
BULLE OGIER
STEPHANE AUDRAN
JEAN-PIERRE CASSEL
JULIEN BERTHEAU
MILENA VUKOTIC
MARIA GABRIELLA MAIONE
CLAUDE PIEPLU
MUNI
FRANÇOIS MAISTRE
PIERRE MAGUELON
MAXENCE MAILFORT

scénario de
LUIS BUNUEL
avec la collaboration de
JEAN-CLAUDE CARRIERE

décors de
PIERRE GUFFROY
Directeur de la Photographie
EDMOND RICHARD
Directeur de la Production
ULLY PICKARD
un film produit par
SERGE SILBERMAN
PANAVISION SPHERIQUE
EASTMANCOLOR
Distribué par 20th Century Fox

UNE PRODUCTION
GREENWICH FILM PRODUCTION

UN FILM DE LUIS BUNUEL

Maîtresse (1976)
US 41 × 27 in. (104 × 69 cm)
Art by Allen Jones

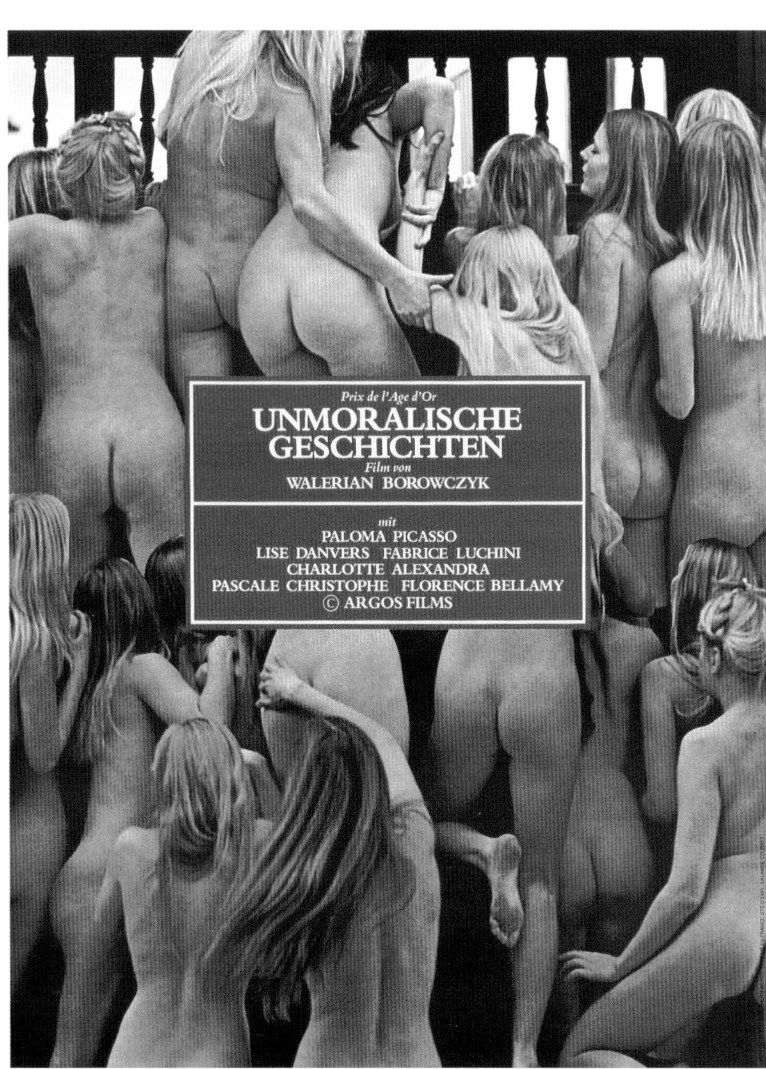

Contes Immoraux / Unmoralische Geschichten (Immoral Tales) (1974)
French 31 × 24 in. (79 × 61 cm)

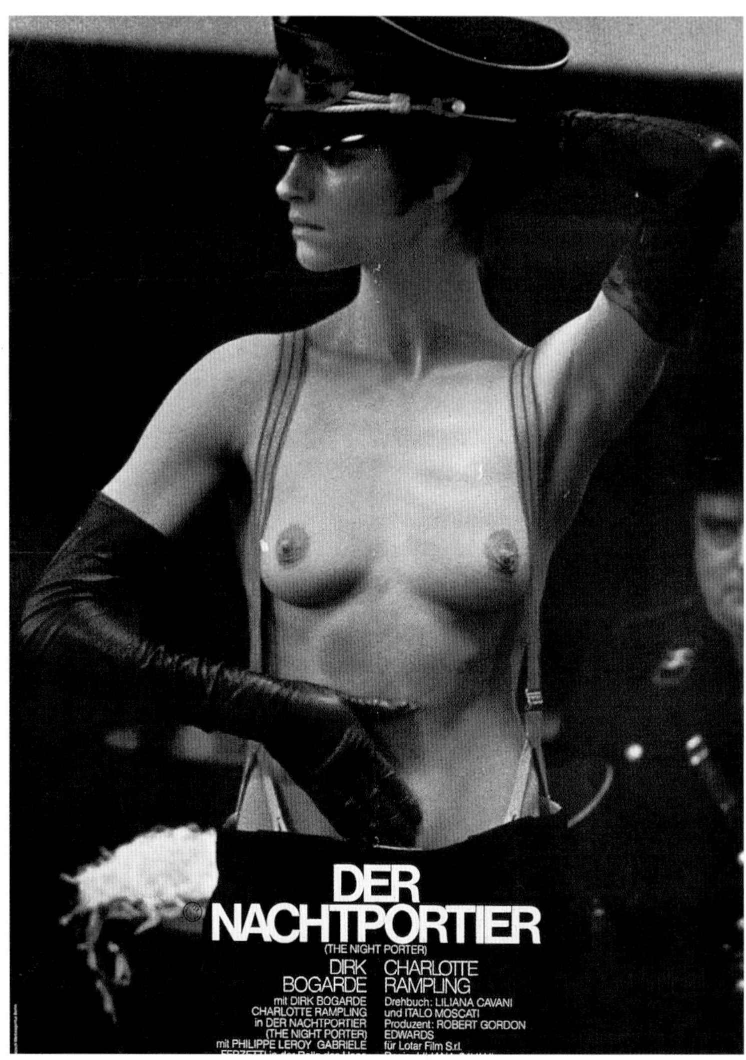

The Night Porter / Der Nachtportier (1974)
German 33 × 23 in. (84 × 58 cm)

GERARD DEPARDIEU

BULLE OGIER

A LOVE STORY ABOUT THE MYSTERIES OF LOVE

She will open your eyes.

A film by Barbet SCHROEDER

MAITRESSE

No one under 17 admitted.

Distributed by Tinc Productions Corp.

The Honeymoon Killers (1970)
US 41 × 27 in. (104 × 69 cm)

L'Homme Qui Aimait Les Femmes / Der Mann, Der Die Frauen Liebte
(US Title: **The Man Who Loved Women**) (1977)
German 33 × 23 in. (84 × 58 cm)

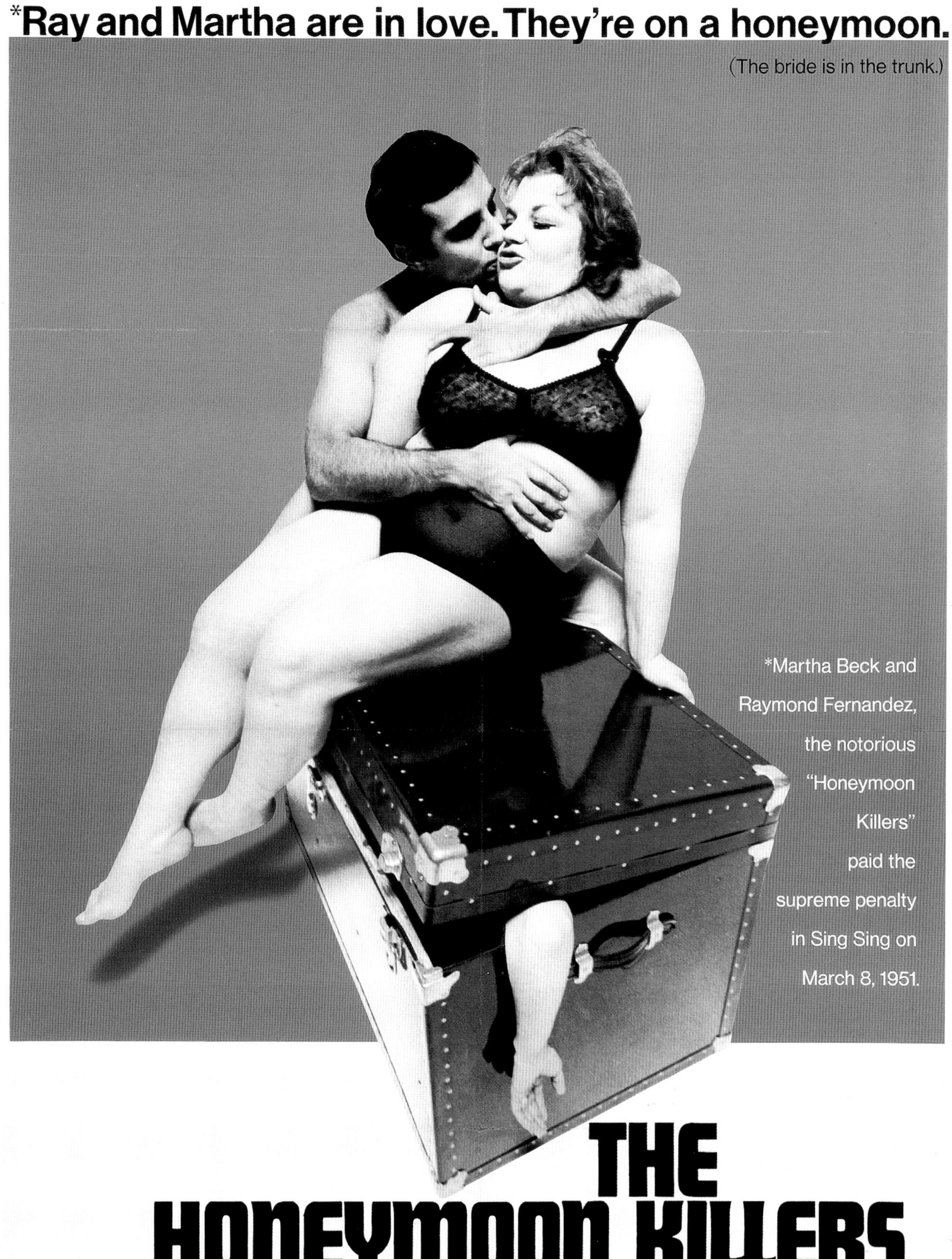
*Ray and Martha are in love. They're on a honeymoon.
(The bride is in the trunk.)
*Martha Beck and Raymond Fernandez, the notorious "Honeymoon Killers" paid the supreme penalty in Sing Sing on March 8, 1951.
THE HONEYMOON KILLERS
R RESTRICTED–PERSONS UNDER 16 NOT ADMITTED, UNLESS ACCOMPANIED BY PARENT OR ADULT GUARDIAN.
A WARREN STEIBEL PRODUCTION Starring SHIRLEY STOLER · TONY LO BIANCO
MARY JANE HIGBY · Written and Directed by LEONARD KASTLE FROM CINERAMA RELEASING CORPORATION
COPYRIGHT © 1970 CINERAMA RELEASING CORPORATION
70/60

Emmanuelle (1975)
US 41 x 27 in. (104 x 69 cm)
Creative Design by Steve Frankfurt

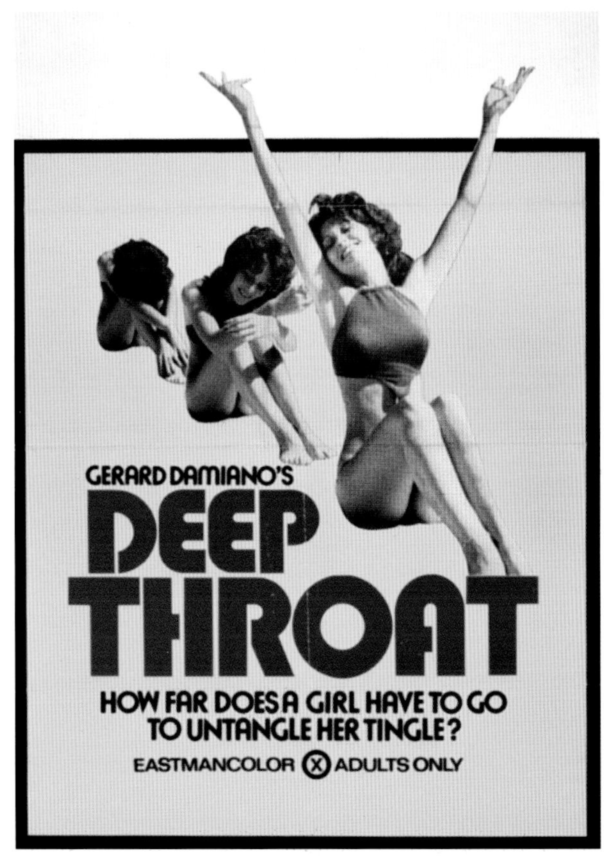

Deep Throat (1974)
US 41 x 27 in. (104 x 69 cm)

Ultimo Tango A Parigi
(Last Tango In Paris) (1973)
Italian 55 x 39 in. (140 x 99 cm)

Emmanuelle

X
was
never
like
this

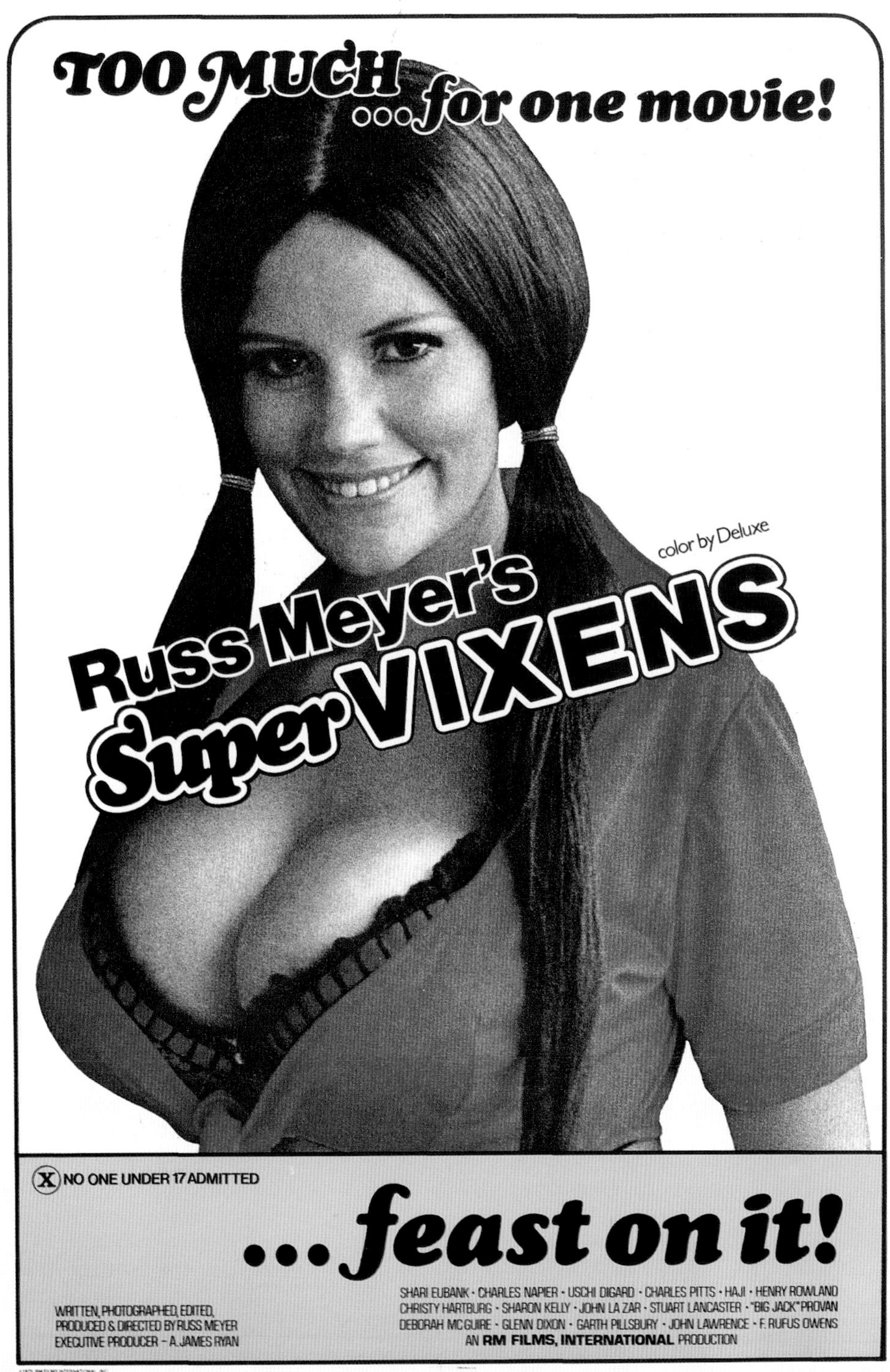

Supervixens (1975)
US 41 × 27 in. (104 × 69 cm)

Fritz The Cat (1972)
US 28 × 18 in. (71 × 46 cm)
Art by Robert Crumb

"We're not rated X
for nothin', baby!"
FRITZ
the CAT
(X)
Jerry Gross Presents • "FRITZ THE CAT" • A Steve Krantz Production • Based upon characters created by R CRUMB • Screenplay by RALPH BAKSHI • Directed by RALPH BAKSHI • Produced by STEVE KRANTZ • A Cinemation Industries Release • Original Soundtrack Album on Fantasy Records
© Aurica Finance Company, N.V. 1972.
He's X rated and animated!

Sleeper (1974)
US 41 × 27 in. (104 × 69 cm)

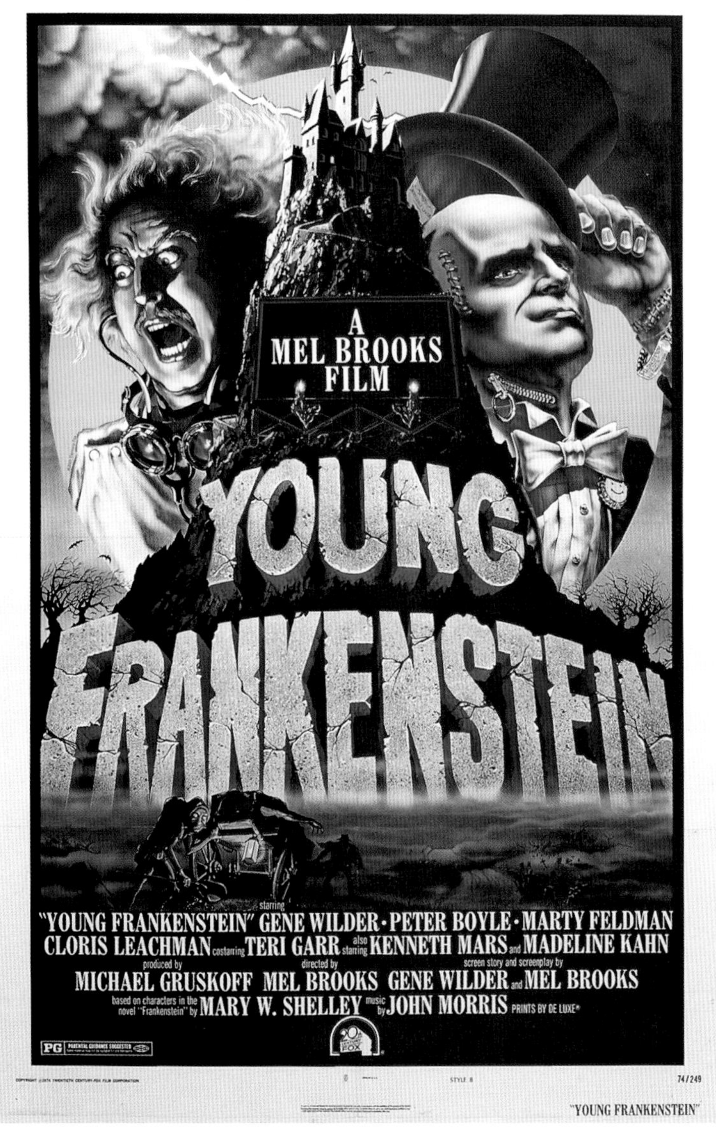

Young Frankenstein (1974)
US 41 × 27 in. (104 × 69 cm)
(Style B)

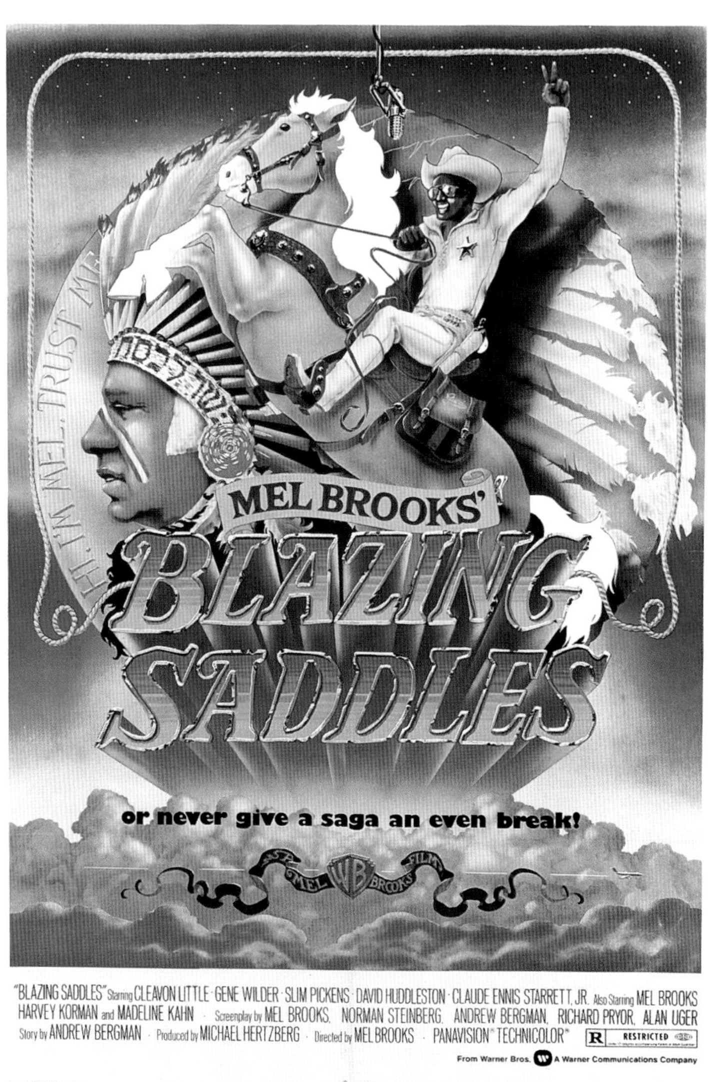

Blazing Saddles (1974)
US 41 × 27 in. (104 × 69 cm)

WOODY ALLEN
TAKES A
NOSTALGIC LOOK
AT THE
FUTURE.
Woody Allen and Diane Keaton
in
"Sleeper"
A JACK ROLLINS–CHARLES H. JOFFE PRODUCTION
Produced by JACK GROSSBERG · Executive Producer CHARLES H. JOFFE
Written by WOODY ALLEN and MARSHALL BRICKMAN · Directed by WOODY ALLEN
PG PARENTAL GUIDANCE SUGGESTED SOME MATERIAL MAY NOT BE SUITABLE FOR PRE-TEENAGERS
United Artists
Entertainment from Transamerica Corporation
Copyright © Jack Rollins and Charles H. Joffe Productions, MCMLXXIII. All Rights Reserved.
74/19

Play It Again Sam (1972)
US 41 × 27 in. (104 × 69 cm)

Annie Hall (1977)
US 41 × 27 in. (104 × 69 cm)

Manhattan (1979)
US 41 × 27 in. (104 × 69 cm)
(Style B)

"It's still the same old story, a fight for love and glory."*
Paramount Pictures presents
An Arthur P. Jacobs Production in association with Rollins-Joffe Productions
"PLAY IT AGAIN, SAM"
A Herbert Ross Film
starring
WOODY ALLEN DIANE KEATON TONY ROBERTS
JERRY LACY and SUSAN ANSPACH co-starring JENNIFER SALT and VIVA as Jennifer
Screenplay by WOODY ALLEN Produced by ARTHUR P. JACOBS Directed by HERBERT ROSS Executive Producer CHARLES H. JOFFE
Based on the play by WOODY ALLEN Produced on the New York stage by David Merrick Music Scored by Billy Goldenberg An APJAC Production Technicolor® A Paramount Picture
SOUNDTRACK ALBUM AVAILABLE ON PARAMOUNT RECORDS
*AS TIME GOES BY by Herman Hupfeld Copyright ©1931 by Harms, Inc. Copyright renewed. All rights reserved. Used by permission of Warner Brothers Music
Paramount
Copyright 1972 by Paramount Pictures Corporation. All rights reserved
72/198

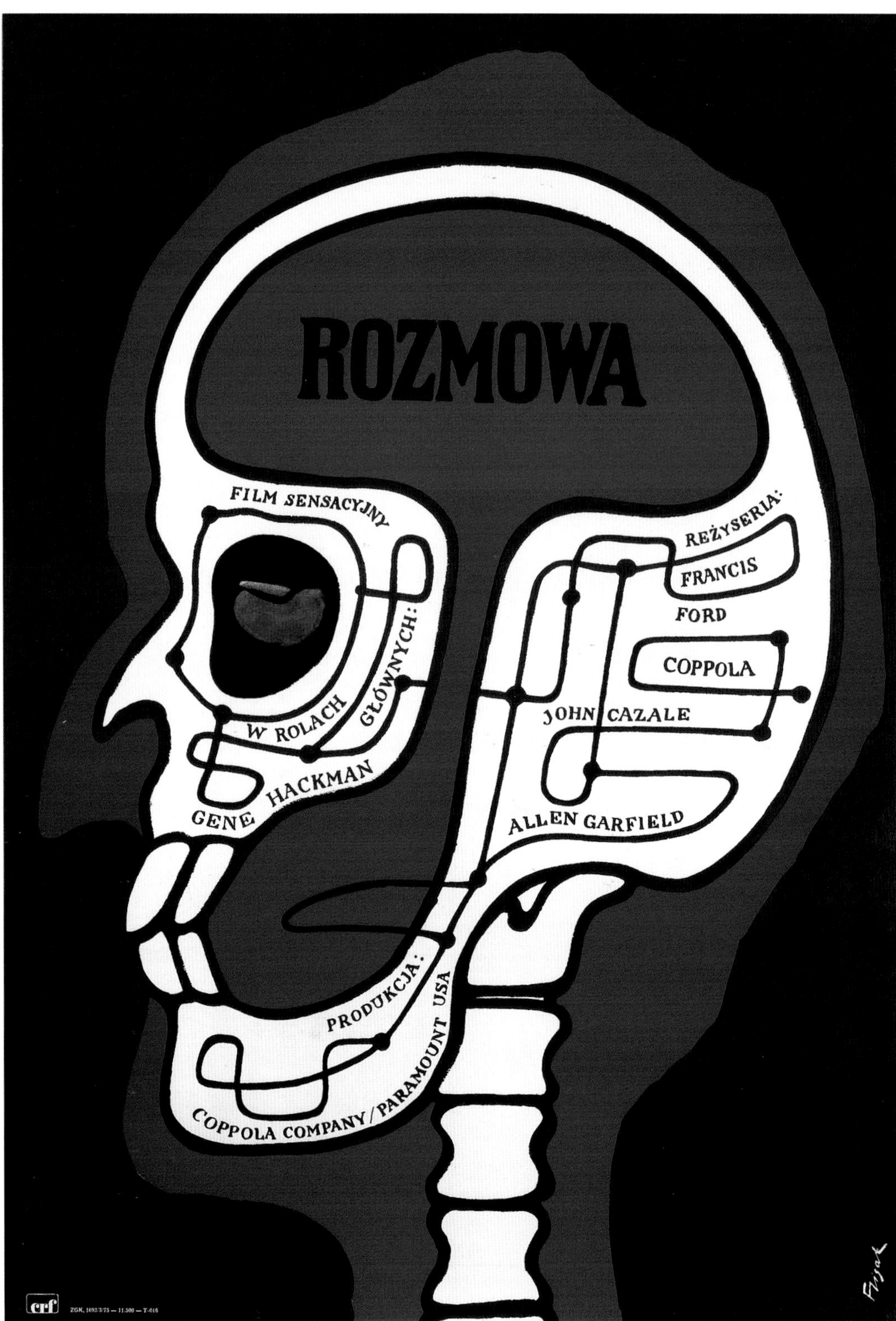

The Conversation / Rozmowa (1974)
Polish 33 x 23 in (84 x 58 cm)
Art by Jerzy Flisak

The Conversation (1974)
US 41 x 27 in. (104 x 69 cm)

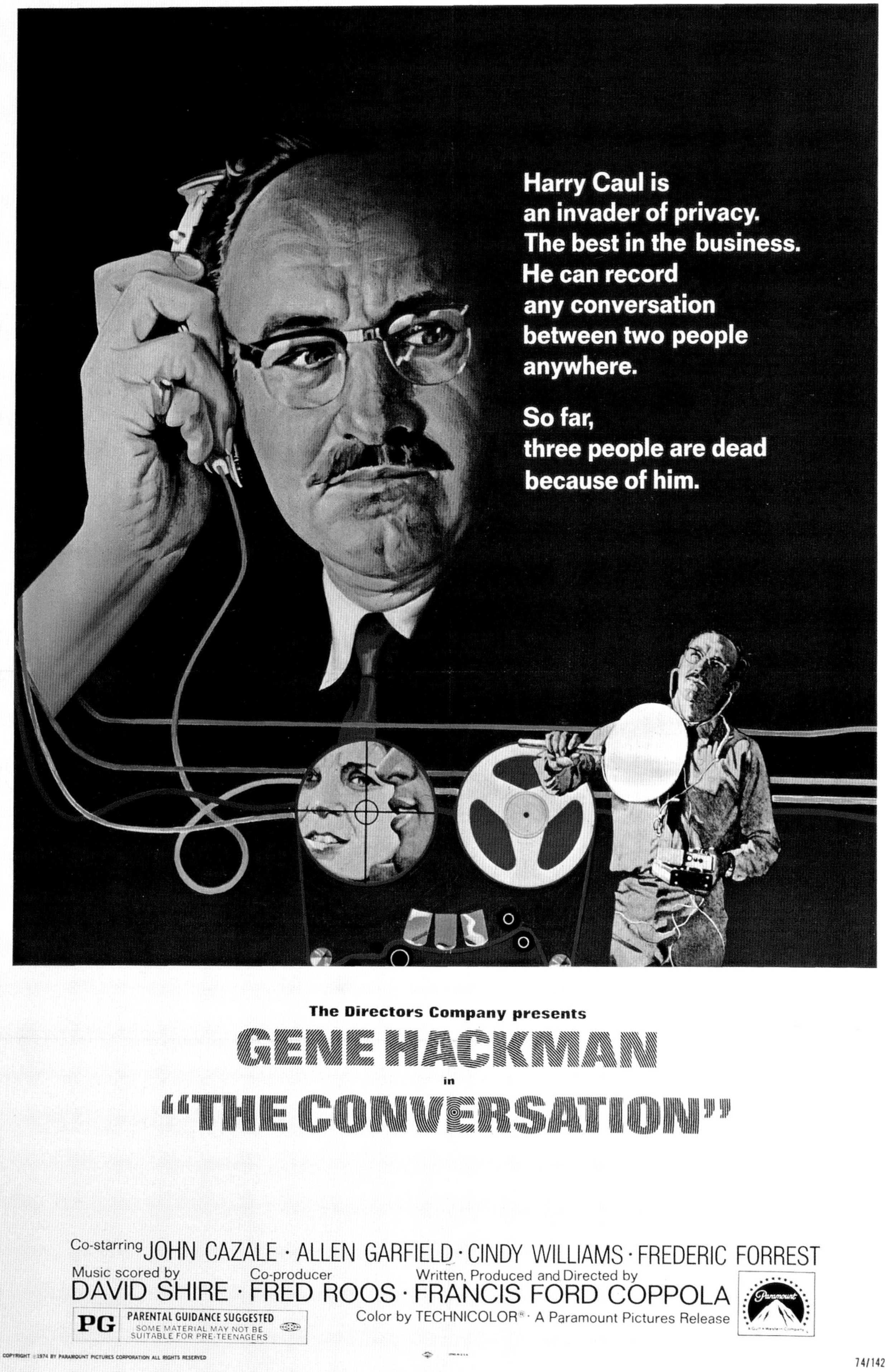

Harry Caul is
an invader of privacy.
The best in the business.
He can record
any conversation
between two people
anywhere.

So far,
three people are dead
because of him.

The Directors Company presents

GENE HACKMAN

in

"THE CONVERSATION"

Co-starring JOHN CAZALE · ALLEN GARFIELD · CINDY WILLIAMS · FREDERIC FORREST

Music scored by DAVID SHIRE · Co-producer FRED ROOS · Written, Produced and Directed by FRANCIS FORD COPPOLA

PG PARENTAL GUIDANCE SUGGESTED SOME MATERIAL MAY NOT BE SUITABLE FOR PRE-TEENAGERS

Color by TECHNICOLOR® · A Paramount Pictures Release

74/142

"THE CONVERSATION"

Klute (1971)
US 41 × 27 in. (104 × 69 cm)

The Parallax View (1974)
US 41 × 27 in. (104 × 69 cm)

All The President's Men (1976)
US 41 × 27 in. (104 × 69 cm)

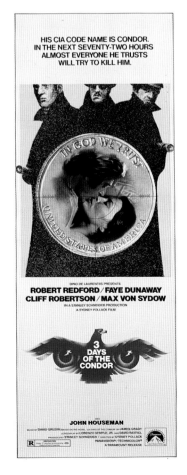

Three Days Of The Condor (1975)
US 36 × 14 in. (91 × 36 cm)

As American as apple pie.

Paramount Pictures Presents

AN ALAN J. PAKULA PRODUCTION

WARREN BEATTY
THE PARALLAX VIEW

Co-starring

HUME CRONYN · WILLIAM DANIELS AND PAULA PRENTISS

Director of Photography GORDON WILLIS · Music Scored by MICHAEL SMALL

Executive Producer GABRIEL KATZKA · Screenplay by DAVID GILER and LORENZO SEMPLE, Jr.

Produced and Directed by ALAN J. PAKULA · PANAVISION® TECHNICOLOR® A Paramount Picture

Taxi Driver (1976)
US 41 × 27 in. (104 × 69 cm)
Art by Guy Peellaert

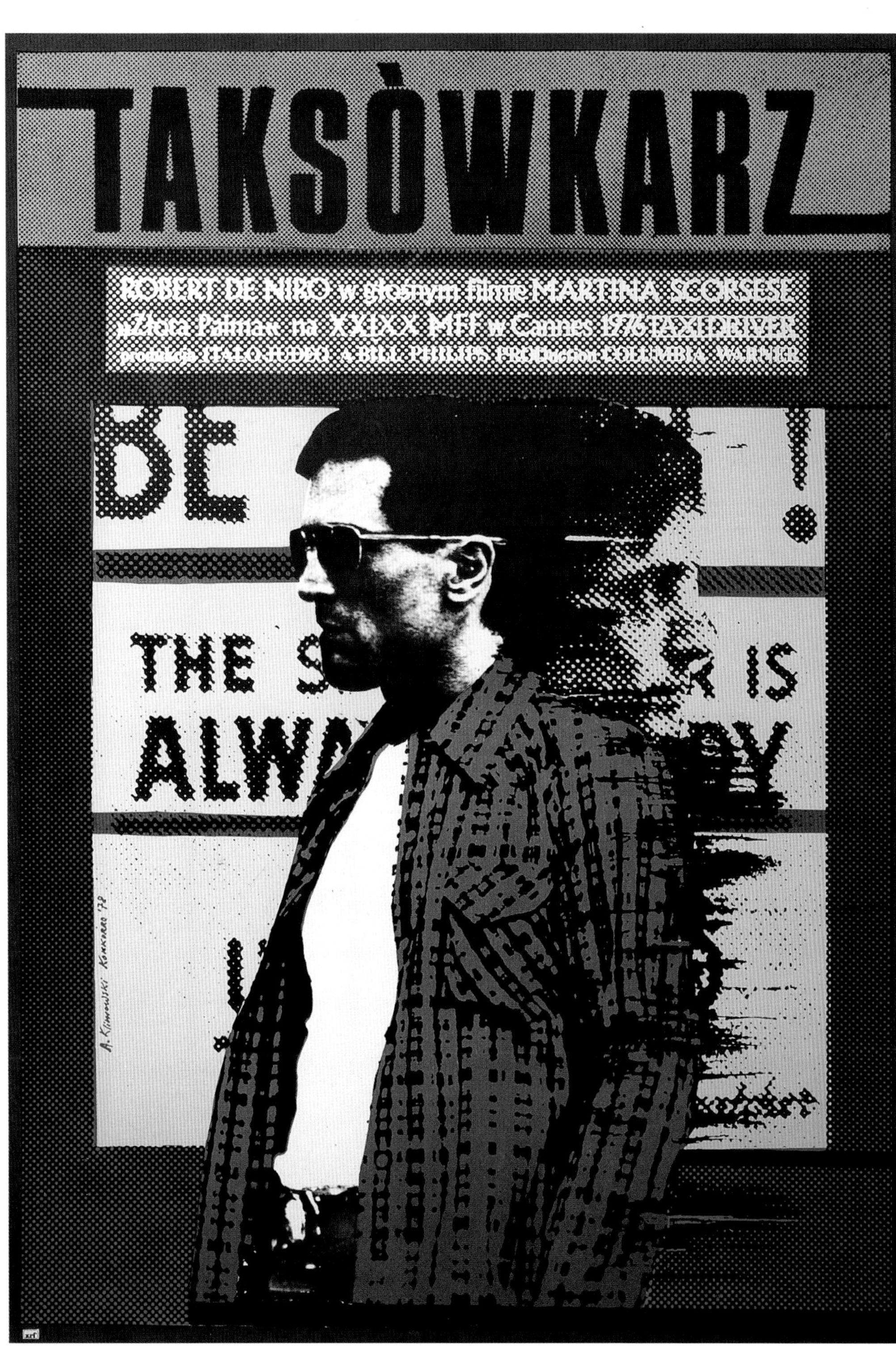

Taxi Driver / Taksowkarz (1976)
Polish 38 × 27 in. (97 × 69 cm)
Art by Andrzej Klimowski

COLUMBIA PICTURES presents
ROBERT DE NIRO
TAXI DRIVER
A BILL/PHILLIPS Production of a MARTIN SCORSESE Film
JODIE FOSTER
ALBERT BROOKS as "Tom"
HARVEY KEITEL
LEONARD HARRIS
PETER BOYLE as "Wizard" and
CYBILL SHEPHERD as "Betsy"
Written by PAUL SCHRADER Music BERNARD HERRMANN Produced by MICHAEL PHILLIPS
and JULIA PHILLIPS Directed by MARTIN SCORSESE Production Services by Devon/Persky-Bright
Columbia Pictures
R
RESTRICTED
Under 17 requires accompanying Parent or Adult Guardian
COPYRIGHT © 1976 COLUMBIA PICTURES INDUSTRIES, INC. ALL RIGHTS RESERVED
76/14

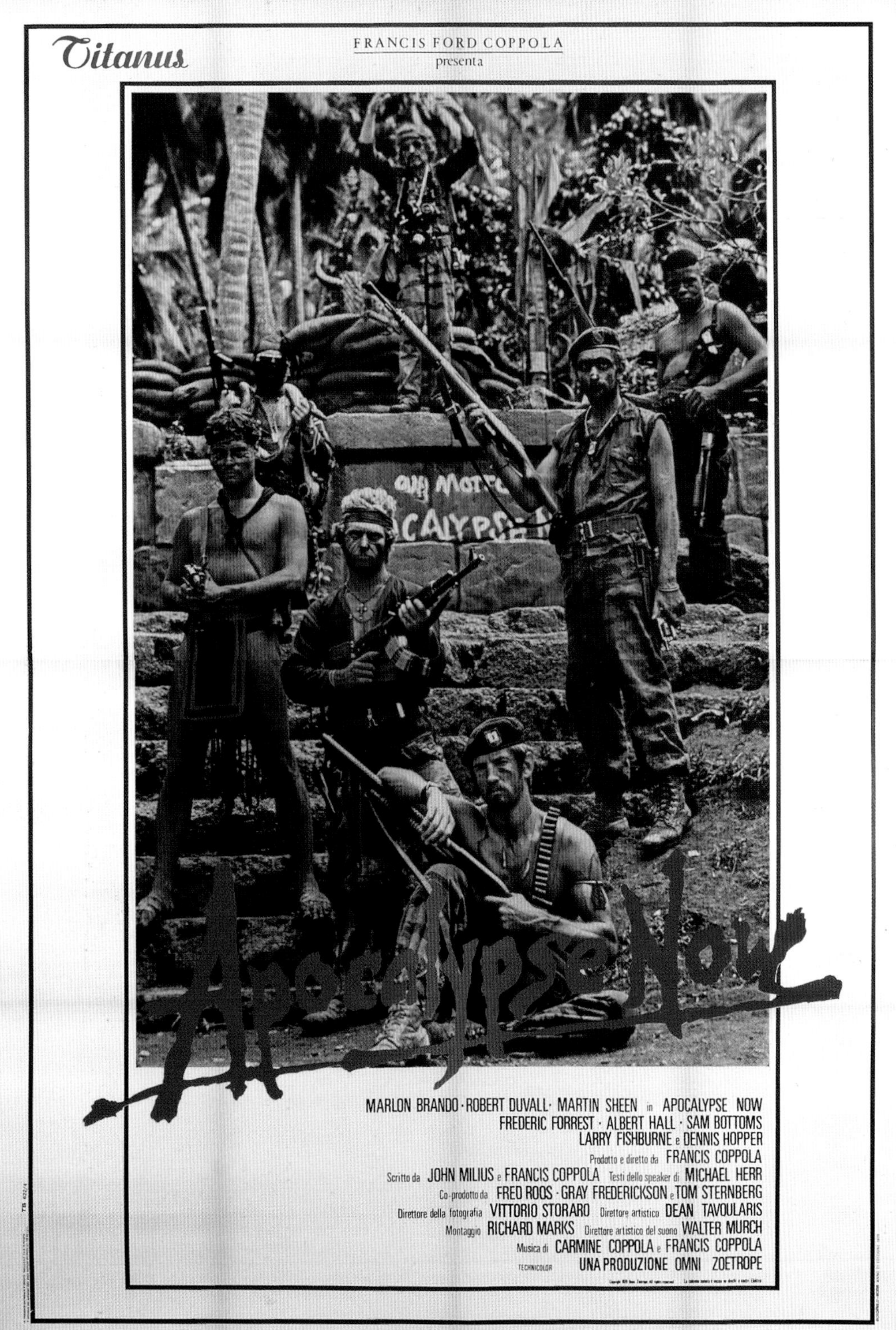

Apocalypse Now (1979)
Italian 79 × 55 in. (201 × 140 cm)
(Style B)

The Deer Hunter (1978)
British International
41 × 27 in. (104 × 69 cm)

THE DEER HUNTER
EMI Films present
ROBERT DE NIRO IN A MICHAEL CIMINO Film THE DEER HUNTER
co-starring
JOHN CAZALE · JOHN SAVAGE · MERYL STREEP · CHRISTOPHER WALKEN
Music composed by STANLEY MYERS · Director of Photography VILMOS ZSIGMOND, A.S.C.
Associate Producers MARION ROSENBERG · JOANN CARELLI · Production Consultant JOANN CARELLI
Story by MICHAEL CIMINO, DERIC WASHBURN and LOUIS GARFINKLE, QUINN K. REDEKER
Screenplay by DERIC WASHBURN · Produced by BARRY SPIKINGS · MICHAEL DEELEY · MICHAEL CIMINO and JOHN PEVERALL
Directed by MICHAEL CIMINO
Technicolor® · Panavision® DOLBY SYSTEM® Stereo Distributed by EMI Films Limited ©1978 by EMI Films, Inc.
EMI

Catch 22 (1970)
US 41 × 27 in. (104 × 69 cm)

Kelly's Heroes (1970)
US 41 × 27 in. (104 × 69 cm)
(Style B)

1941 (1979)
US 41 × 27 in. (104 × 69 cm)
(Advance)

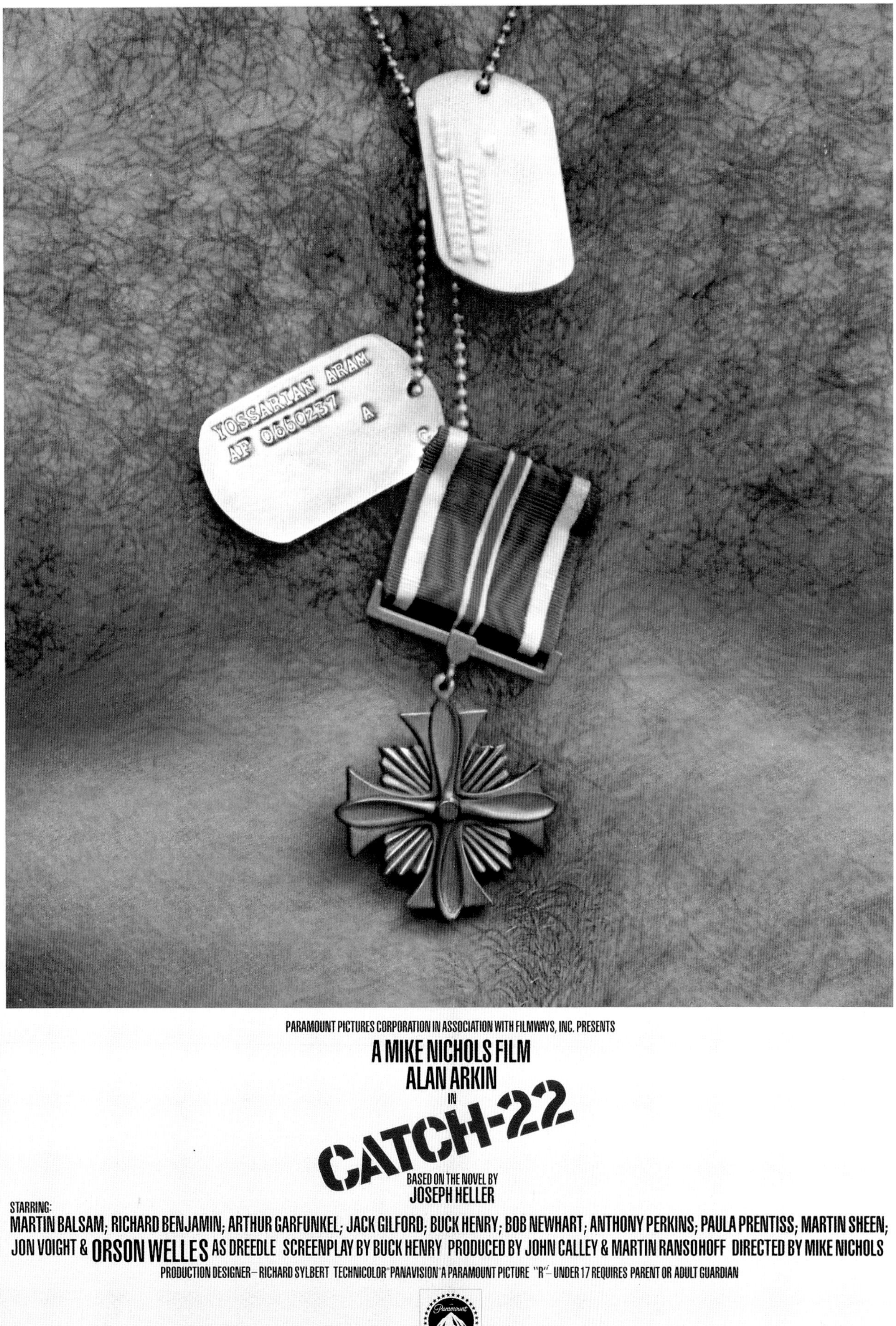

PARAMOUNT PICTURES CORPORATION IN ASSOCIATION WITH FILMWAYS, INC. PRESENTS

A MIKE NICHOLS FILM

ALAN ARKIN

IN

CATCH-22

BASED ON THE NOVEL BY

JOSEPH HELLER

STARRING:

MARTIN BALSAM; RICHARD BENJAMIN; ARTHUR GARFUNKEL; JACK GILFORD; BUCK HENRY; BOB NEWHART; ANTHONY PERKINS; PAULA PRENTISS; MARTIN SHEEN; JON VOIGHT & **ORSON WELLES** AS DREEDLE SCREENPLAY BY BUCK HENRY PRODUCED BY JOHN CALLEY & MARTIN RANSOHOFF DIRECTED BY MIKE NICHOLS

PRODUCTION DESIGNER – RICHARD SYLBERT TECHNICOLOR® PANAVISION® A PARAMOUNT PICTURE "R" – UNDER 17 REQUIRES PARENT OR ADULT GUARDIAN

70/188

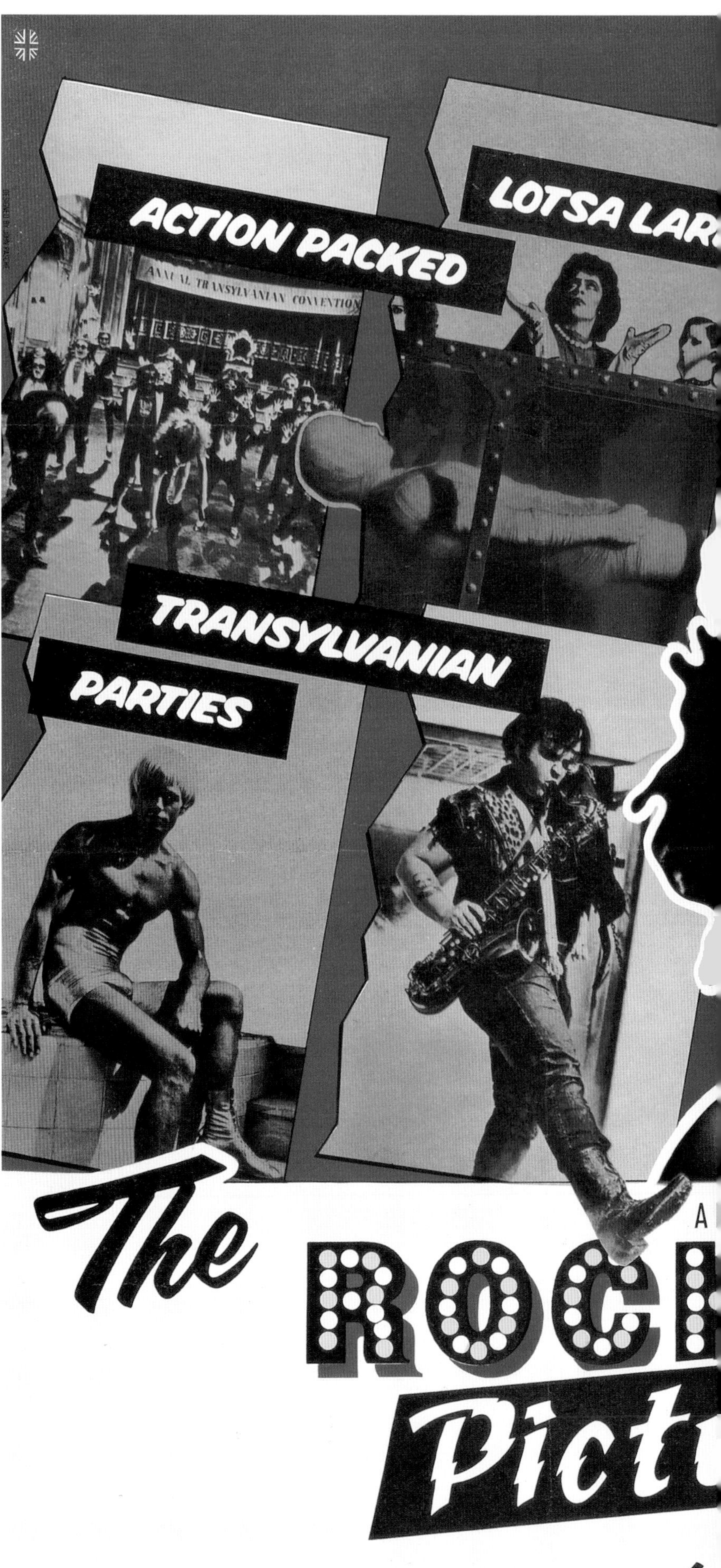

The Rocky Horror Picture Show (1975)
British 30 × 40 in. (76 × 102 cm)
Art by John Pasche

G SEX
GORGEOUS GALS
THRILLS & CHILLS
ROMANCE
Plus 18 Great Songs
TWENTIETH CENTURY FOX PRESENTS
L WHITE–LOU ADLER PRODUCTION
Y HORROR
re SHOW AA
ical Dream Come True
LEY
COMPANY
ASSOCIATE PRODUCER JOHN GOLDSTONE
EXECUTIVE PRODUCER LOU ADLER
DIRECTED BY JIM SHARMAN
PRODUCED BY MICHAEL WHITE
'THE ROCKY HORROR PICTURE SHOW'. AA
STARRING
TIM CURRY • SUSAN SARANDON • BARRY BOSTWICK
RICHARD O'BRIEN • PATRICIA QUINN • LITTLE NELL
JONATHAN ADAMS • PETER HINWOOD • MEATLOAF • CHARLES GRAY
EASTMAN COLOUR RELEASED BY FOX-RANK DISTRIBUTORS
ORIGINAL FILM SOUNDTRACK LP ON ODE 78332

Woodstock (1970)
German 24 × 17 in. (61 × 43 cm)
Art by Richard Amsel

Woodstock (1970)
British 30 × 40 in. (76 × 102 cm)

Woodstock (1970)
US 41 × 27 in. (104 × 69 cm)
(Advance)

woodstock

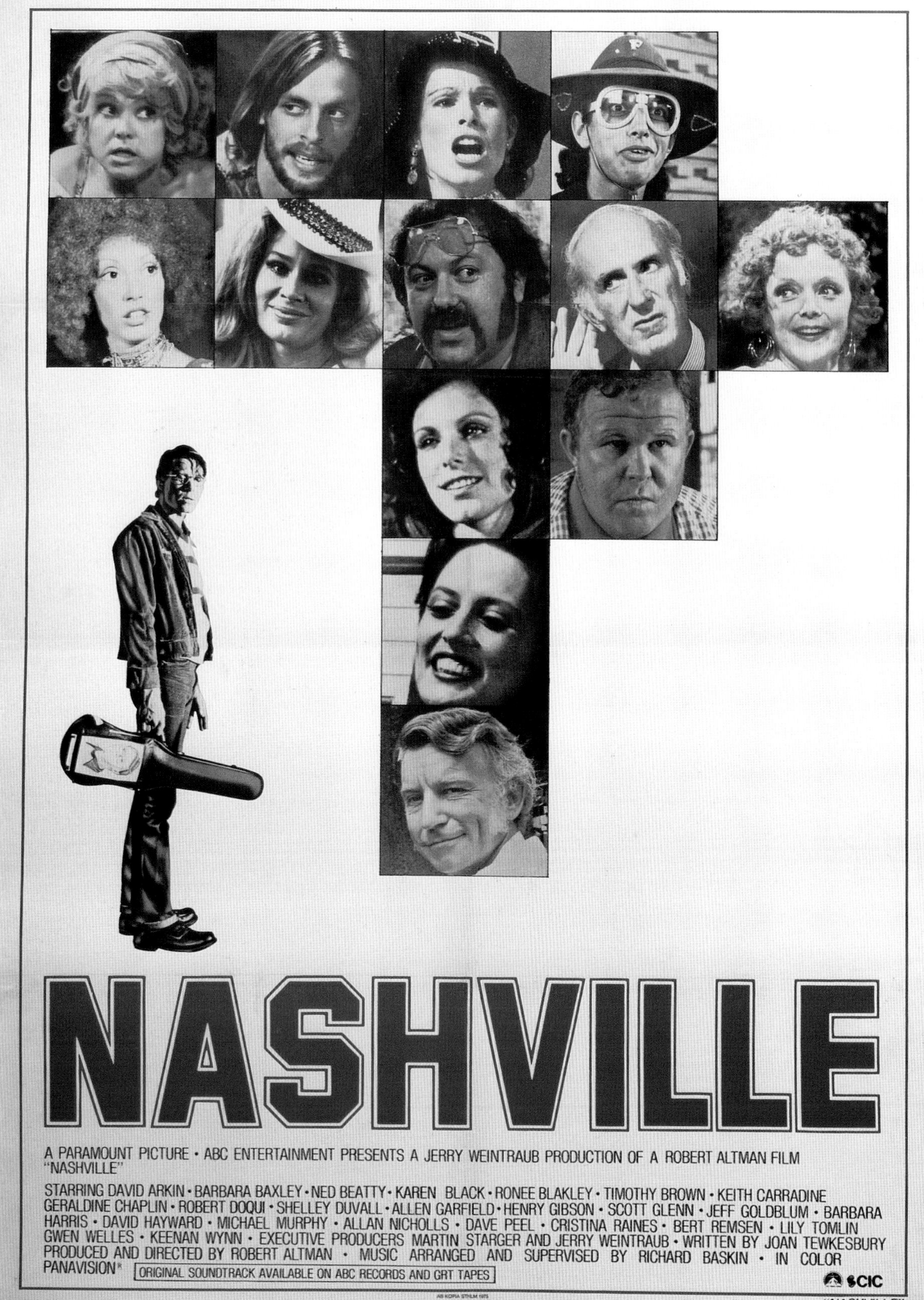

Nashville (1975)
US International
42 × 28 in. (107 × 71 cm)

Elvis On Tour (1972)
US 41 × 27 in. (104 × 69 cm)

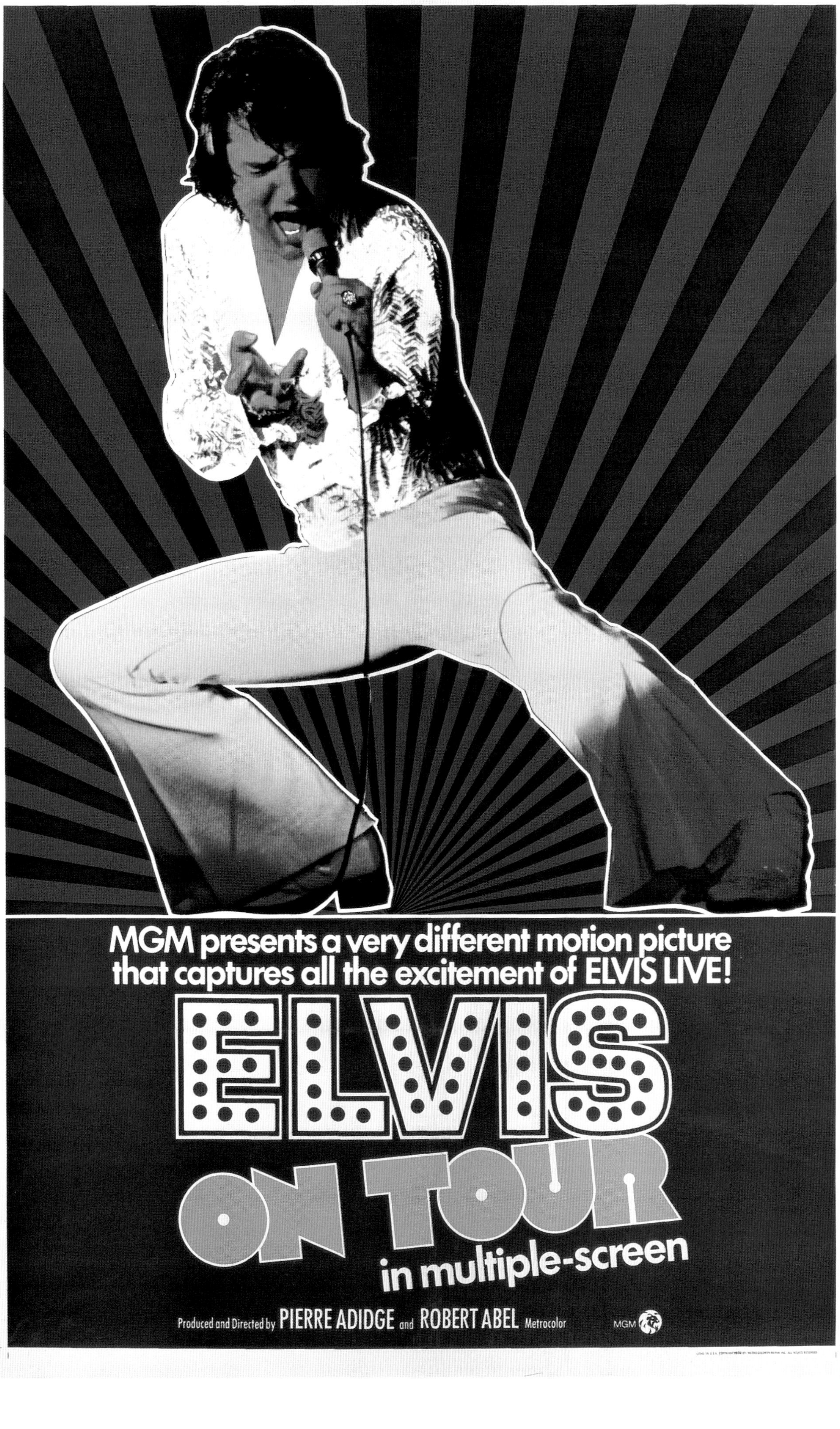

MGM presents a very different motion picture
that captures all the excitement of ELVIS LIVE!

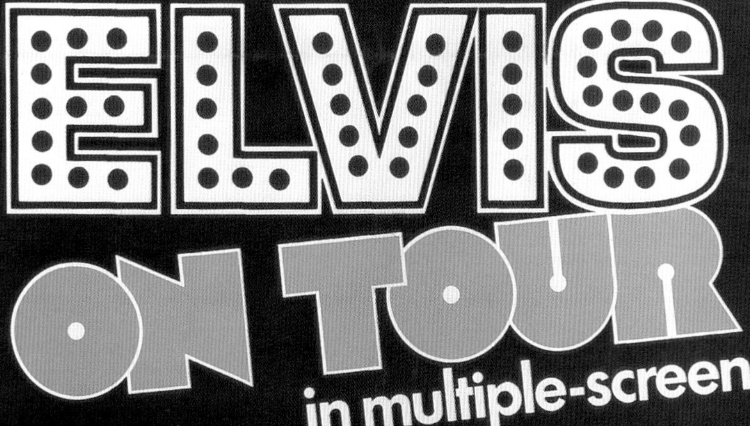

in multiple-screen

Produced and Directed by PIERRE ADIDGE and ROBERT ABEL Metrocolor

Saturday Night Fever (1977)
US 41 × 27 in. (104 × 69 cm)

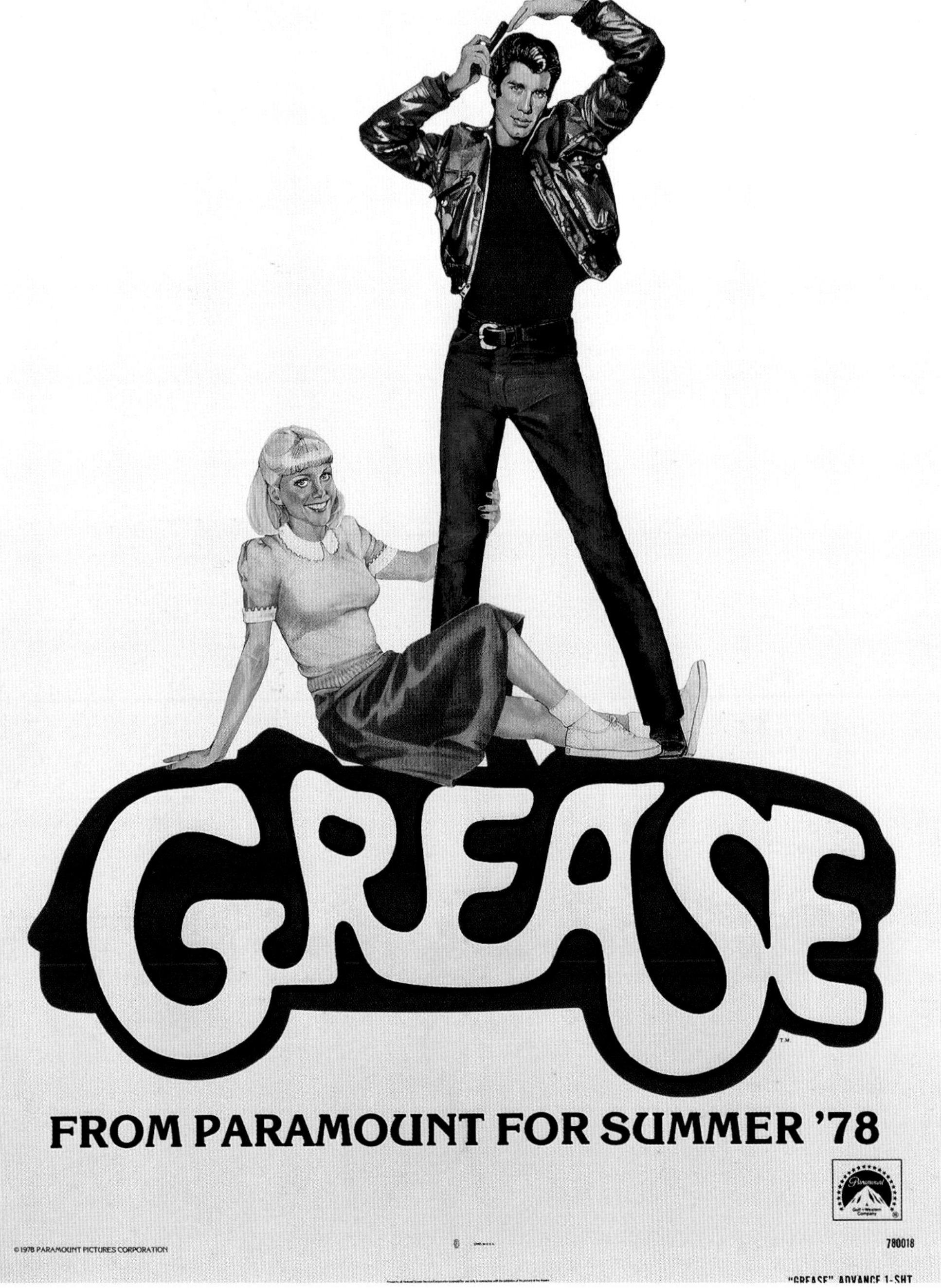

Grease (1978)
US 41 × 27 in. (104 × 69 cm)
(Advance)

Where do you go when the record is over...
SATURDAY NIGHT FEVER
PARAMOUNT PICTURES PRESENTS A ROBERT STIGWOOD PRODUCTION
JOHN TRAVOLTA KAREN GORNEY "SATURDAY NIGHT FEVER"
Screenplay by NORMAN WEXLER Directed by JOHN BADHAM
Executive Producer KEVIN McCORMICK Produced by ROBERT STIGWOOD
Original music written and performed by the Bee Gees Soundtrack album available on RSO Records Read the Bantam Paperback
DOLBY SYSTEM
©1977 Paramount Pictures Corporation. All Rights Reserved
A Paramount Picture
770134

Gimme Shelter (1970)
US 41 × 27 in. (104 × 69 cm)

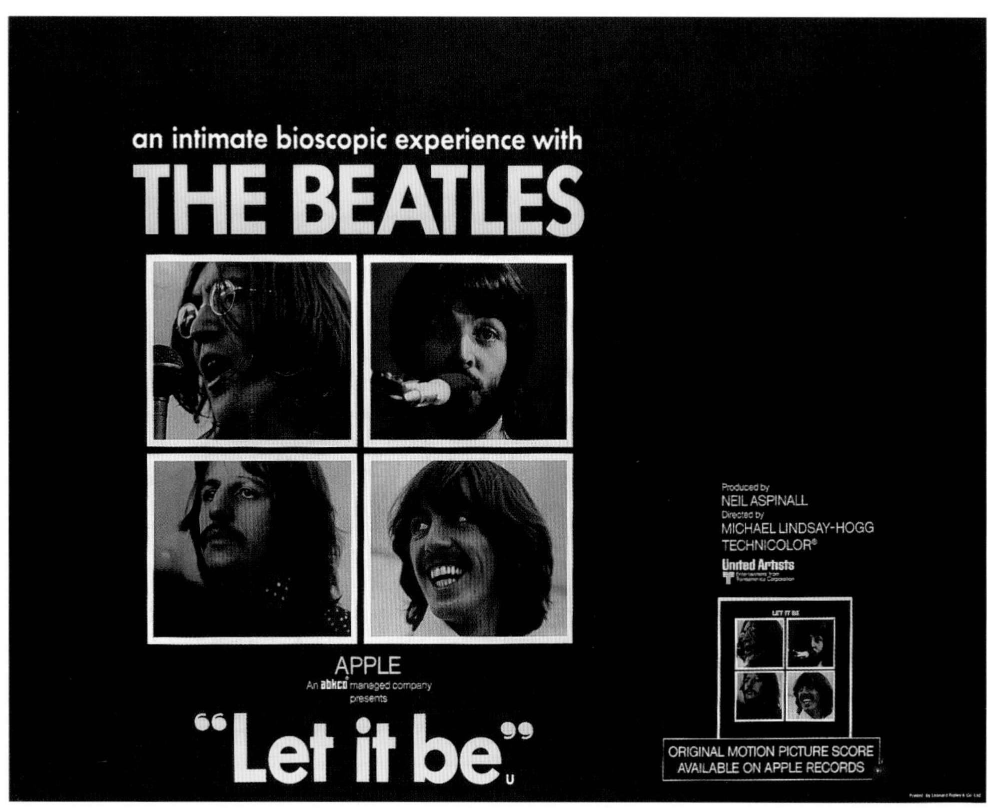

Let It Be (1970)
British 30 × 40 in. (76 × 102 cm)

A Film About Jimi Hendrix (1973)
US 41 × 27 in. (104 × 69 cm)

THE MUSIC THAT THRILLED THE WORLD...
AND THE KILLING THAT STUNNED IT!

The Rolling Stones
Gimme Shelter
DIRECTED BY DAVID MAYSLES, ALBERT MAYSLES, CHARLOTTE ZWERIN · A MAYSLES FILMS, INC. PRODUCTION
DISTRIBUTED BY 20TH CENTURY-FOX FILM CORPORATION

The Great Rock 'n' Roll Swindle (1979)
British 30 x 40 in. (76 x 102 cm)
Art by M. Hirsch

ates its audience

BOYDS CO. & VIRGIN FILMS LIMITED
IN ASSOCIATION WITH MATRIXBEST LIMITED
PRESENT

THE GREAT ROCK 'N' ROLL SWINDLE

X

WITH MUSIC BY

SEX PISTOLS

WRITTEN & DIRECTED BY
JULIEN TEMPLE

EXECUTIVE PRODUCERS
JEREMY THOMAS & DON BOYD

WITH
Mary Millington
LIZ FRAZER
SPECIAL GUEST APPEARANCE
THE BLACK ARABS
Irene Handl

VE JONES
Malcolm McLaren
Helen of Troy

RELEASED BY VIRGIN FILMS

Sound track album available on Virgin Records V2168, cassette TCV2168.
Read Michael Moorcock's newspaper of the book of the novel of the film of the record of the group etc. available from Virgin Books.

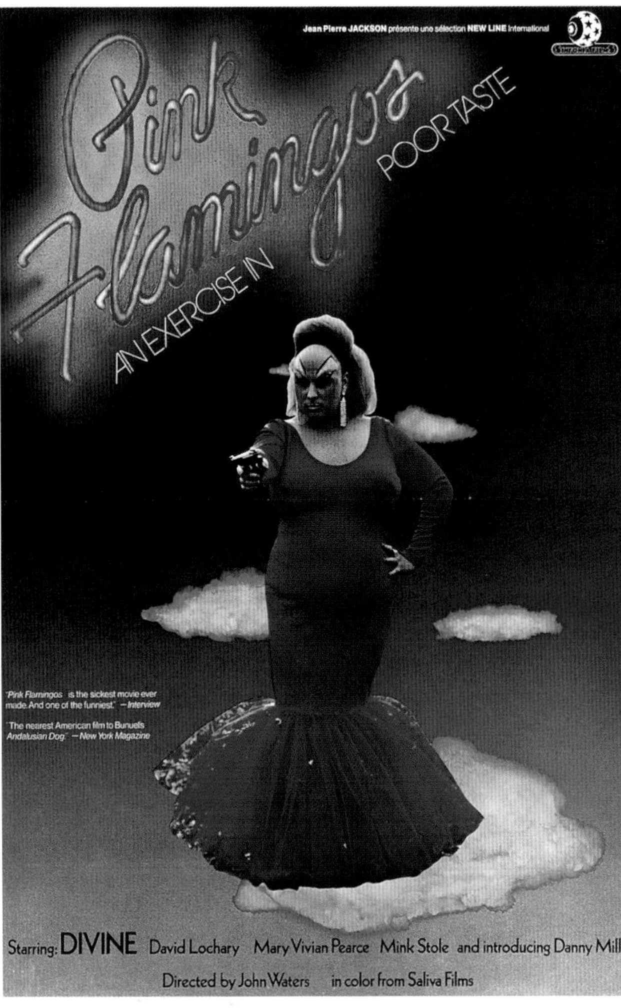

Pink Flamingos (1972)
US 22 × 15 in. (56 × 38 cm)

Eraserhead (1977)
US 22 × 17 in. (56 × 43 cm)

Desperate Living / Punk Story (1977)
Italian 55 × 39 in. (140 × 99 cm)
Art by Tino Avelli

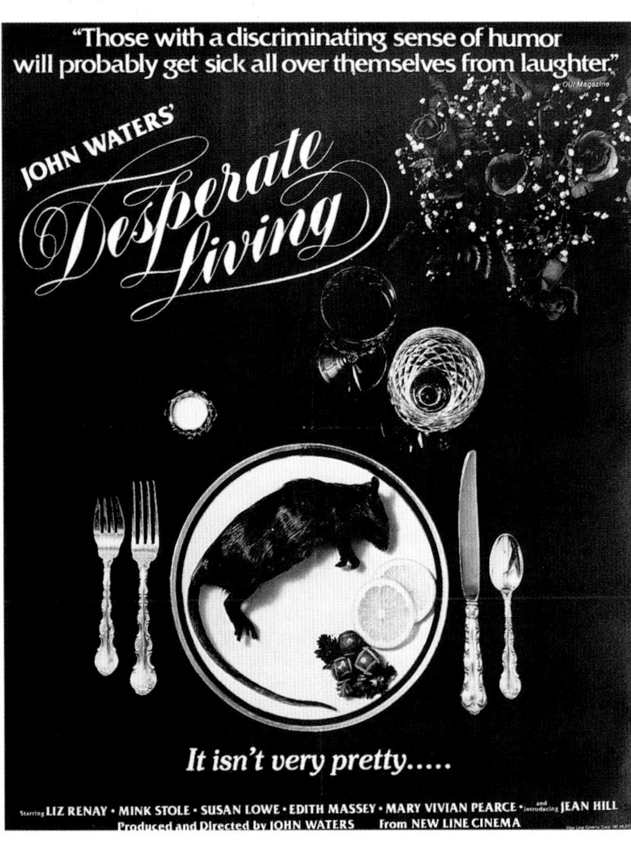

Desperate Living (1977)
US 21 × 17 in. (53 × 43 cm)
Photograph by Peter Hujar

ERASERHEAD
A FILM BY DAVID LYNCH
A Libra Films RELEASE

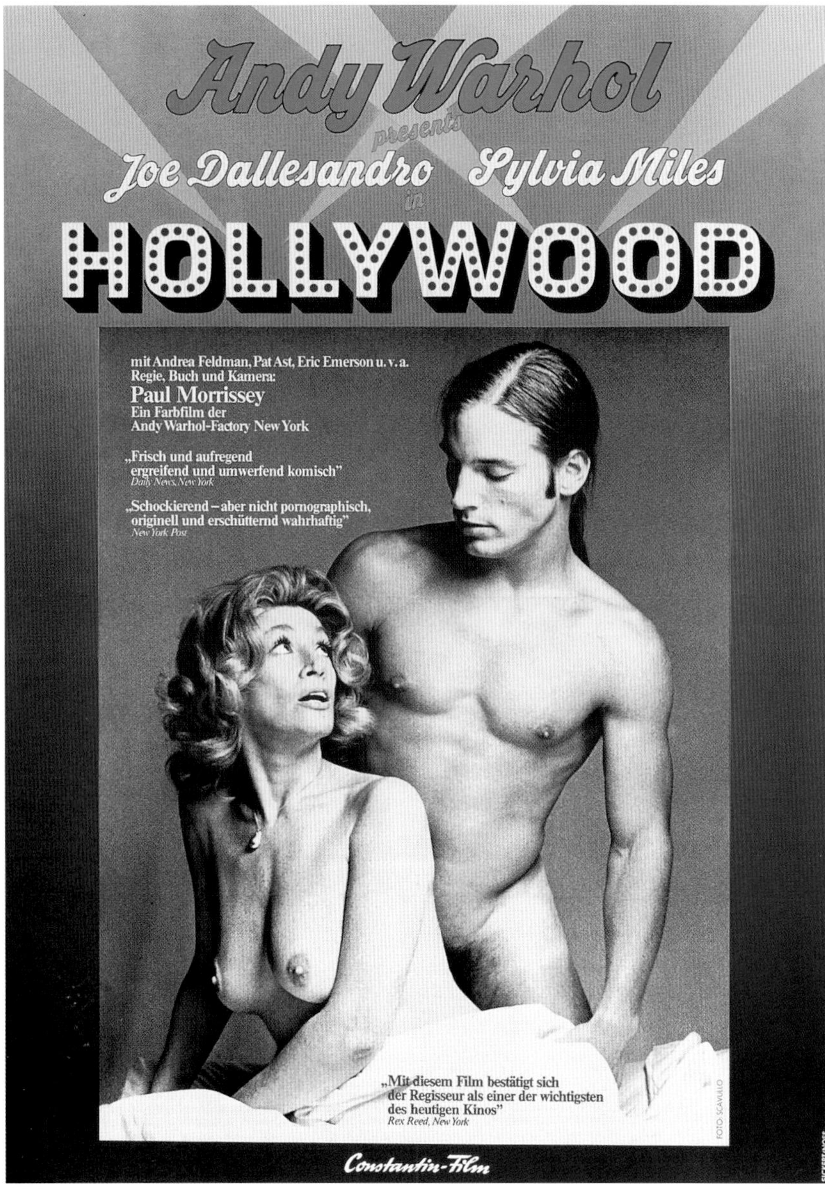

Heat / Hollywood (1971)
German 33 × 23 in. (84 × 58 cm)
(Uncensored Version)
Photograph by Scavullo

Trash (1970)
US 41 × 27 in. (104 × 69 cm)
Photograph by Jack Mitchell

Andy Warhol's Frankenstein (1974)
US 41 × 27 in. (104 × 69 cm)

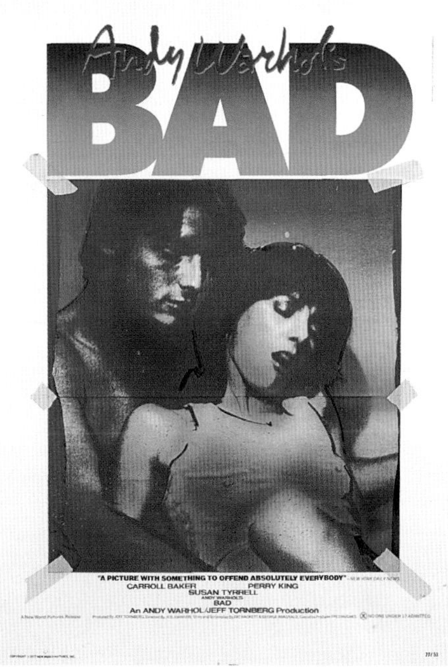

Andy Warhol's Bad (1977)
US 41 × 27 in. (104 × 69 cm)
Art by John Van Hamersveld

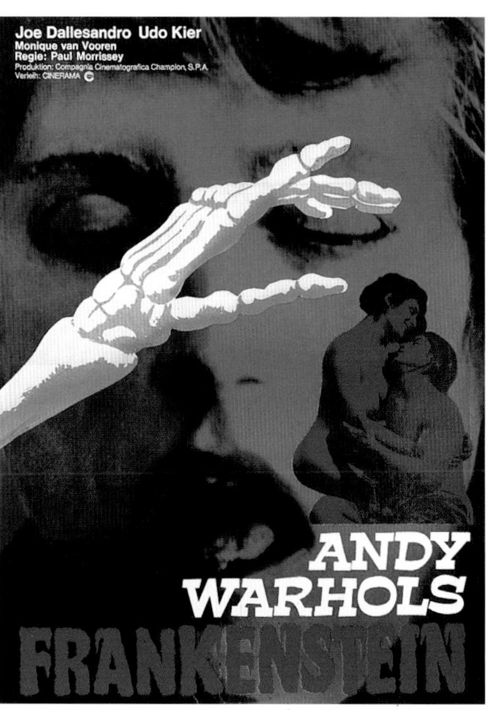

Andy Warhol's Frankenstein (1974)
German 33 × 23 in. (84 × 58 cm)

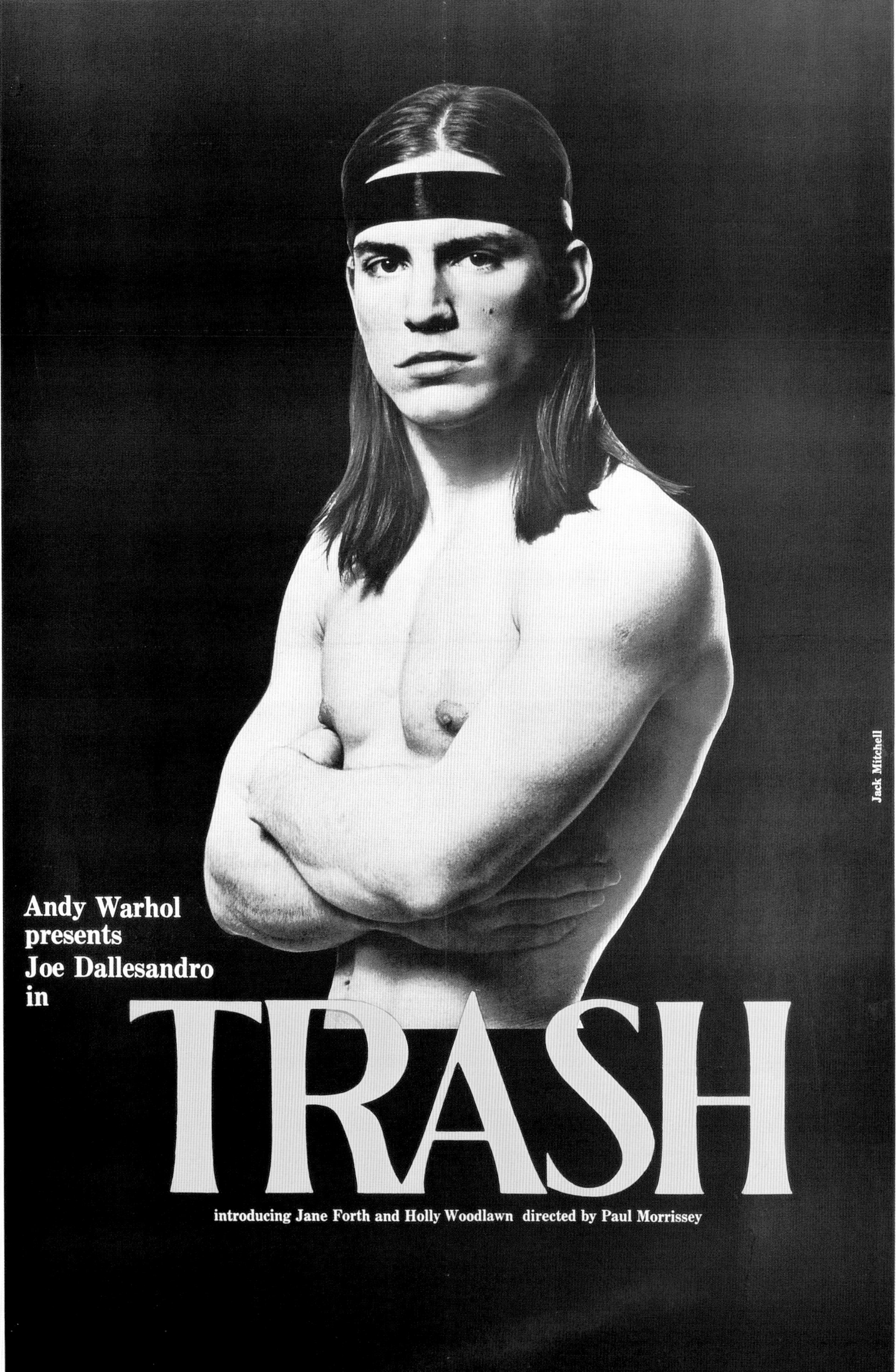
Andy Warhol
presents
Joe Dallesandro
in
TRASH
introducing Jane Forth and Holly Woodlawn directed by Paul Morrissey
Jack Mitchell

Halloween (1978)
US 41 × 27 in. (104 × 69 cm)

Carrie (1976)
US 41 × 27 in. (104 × 69 cm)

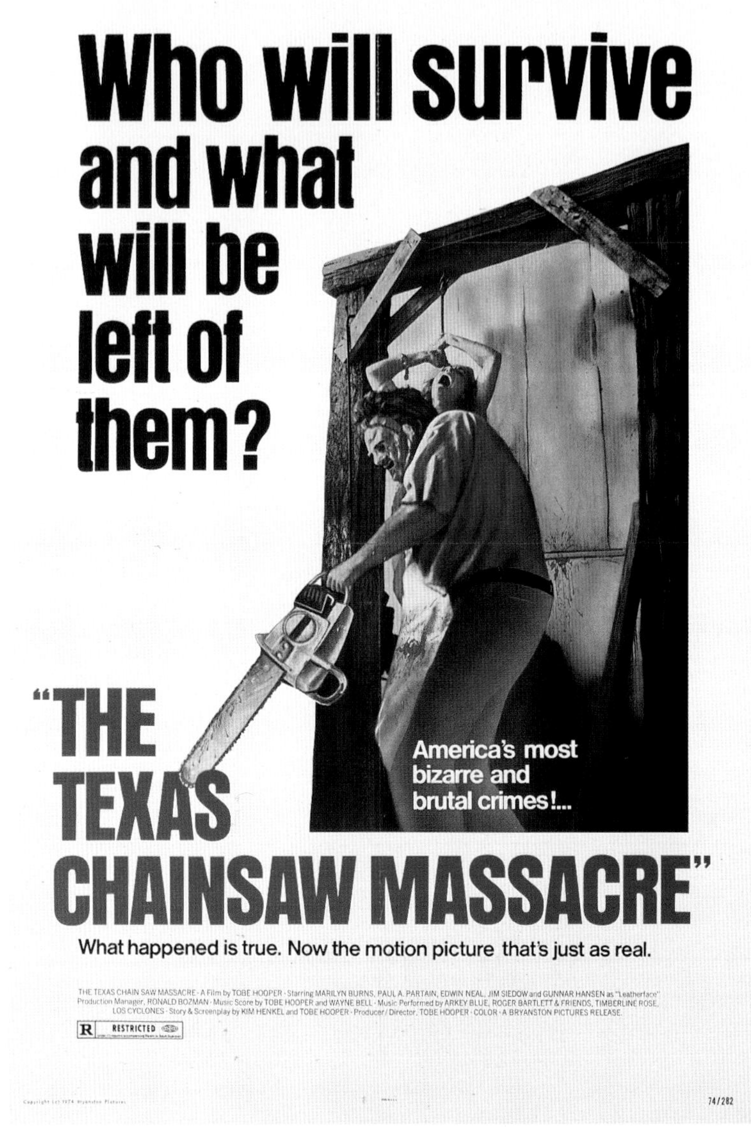

The Texas Chainsaw Massacre (1974)
US 41 × 27 in. (104 × 69 cm)

HALLOWEEN
The Night He Came Home!
MOUSTAPHA AKKAD PRESENTS DONALD PLEASENCE IN JOHN CARPENTER'S "HALLOWEEN"
WITH JAMIE LEE CURTIS, P.J. SOLES, NANCY LOOMIS · WRITTEN BY JOHN CARPENTER AND DEBRA HILL
EXECUTIVE PRODUCER IRWIN YABLANS · DIRECTED BY JOHN CARPENTER · PRODUCED BY DEBRA HILL
PANAVISION
A COMPASS INTERNATIONAL RELEASE
R RESTRICTED

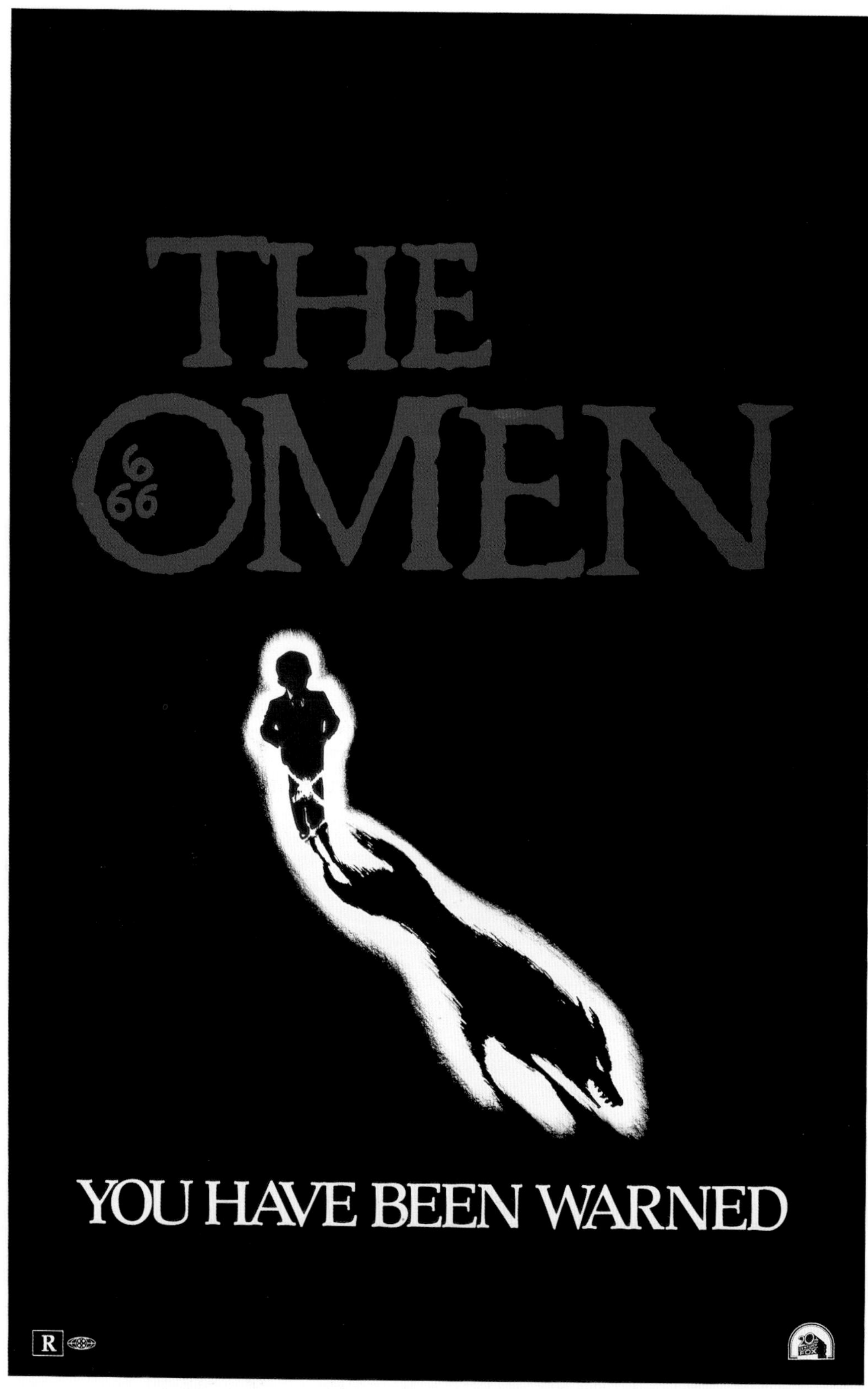

The Omen (1976)
US 41 × 27 in. (104 × 69 cm)
(Advance)

The Exorcist (1974)
US 41 × 27 in. (104 × 69 cm)

THE EXORCIST

Directed by WILLIAM FRIEDKIN

Something almost beyond comprehension is happening to a girl on this street, in this house ...and a man has been sent for as a last resort. This man is The Exorcist.

ELLEN BURSTYN · MAX VON SYDOW · LEE J. COBB
KITTY WINN · JACK MacGOWRAN JASON MILLER as Father Karras
LINDA BLAIR as Regan · Produced by WILLIAM PETER BLATTY
Executive Producer NOEL MARSHALL · Screenplay by WILLIAM PETER BLATTY based on his novel
From Warner Bros.  A Warner Communications Company  R RESTRICTED Under 17 requires accompanying Parent or Adult Guardian

74/40

THE EXORCIST

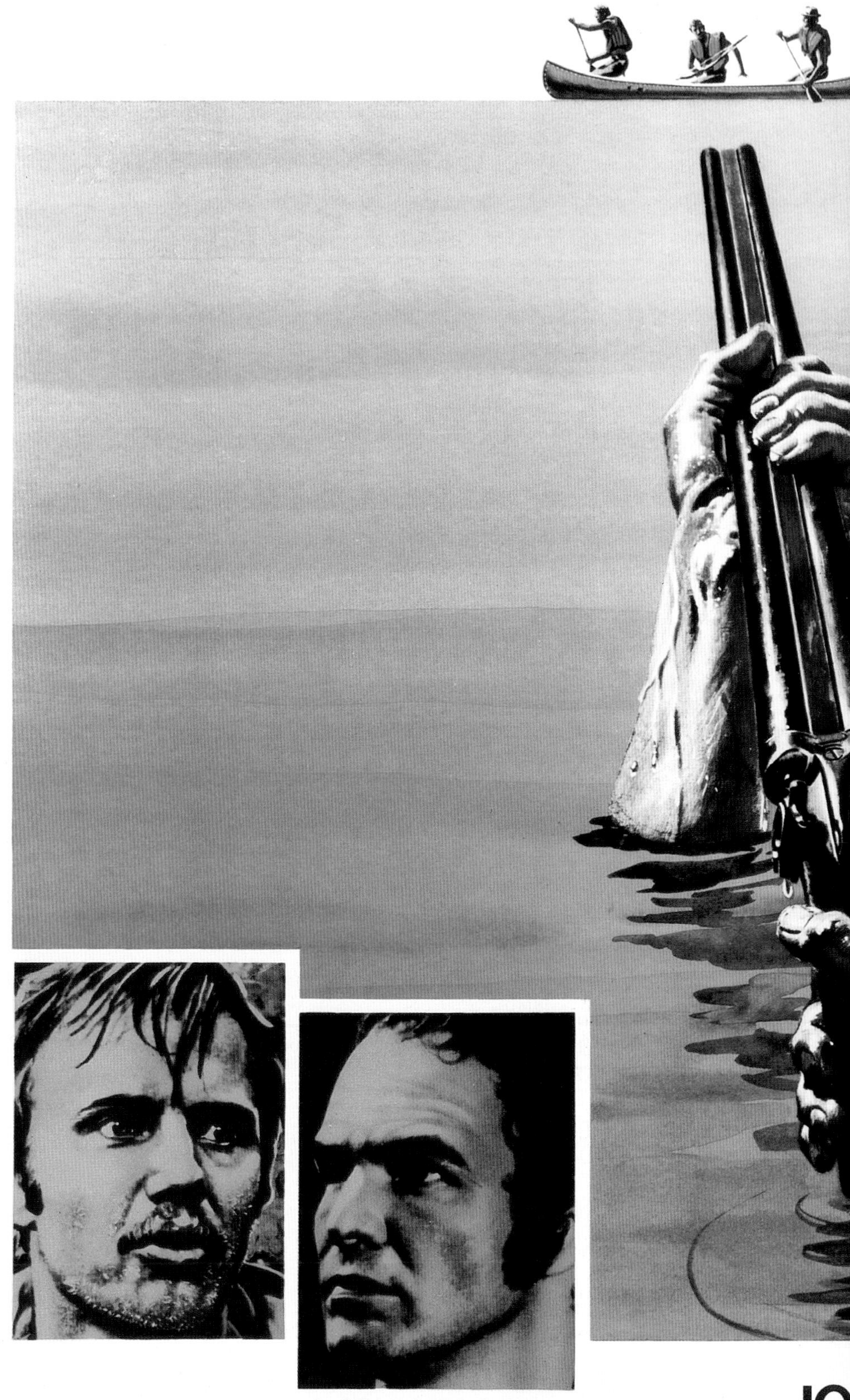

Deliverance (1972)
British 30 × 40 in. (76 × 102 cm)

Where does the camping trip end...

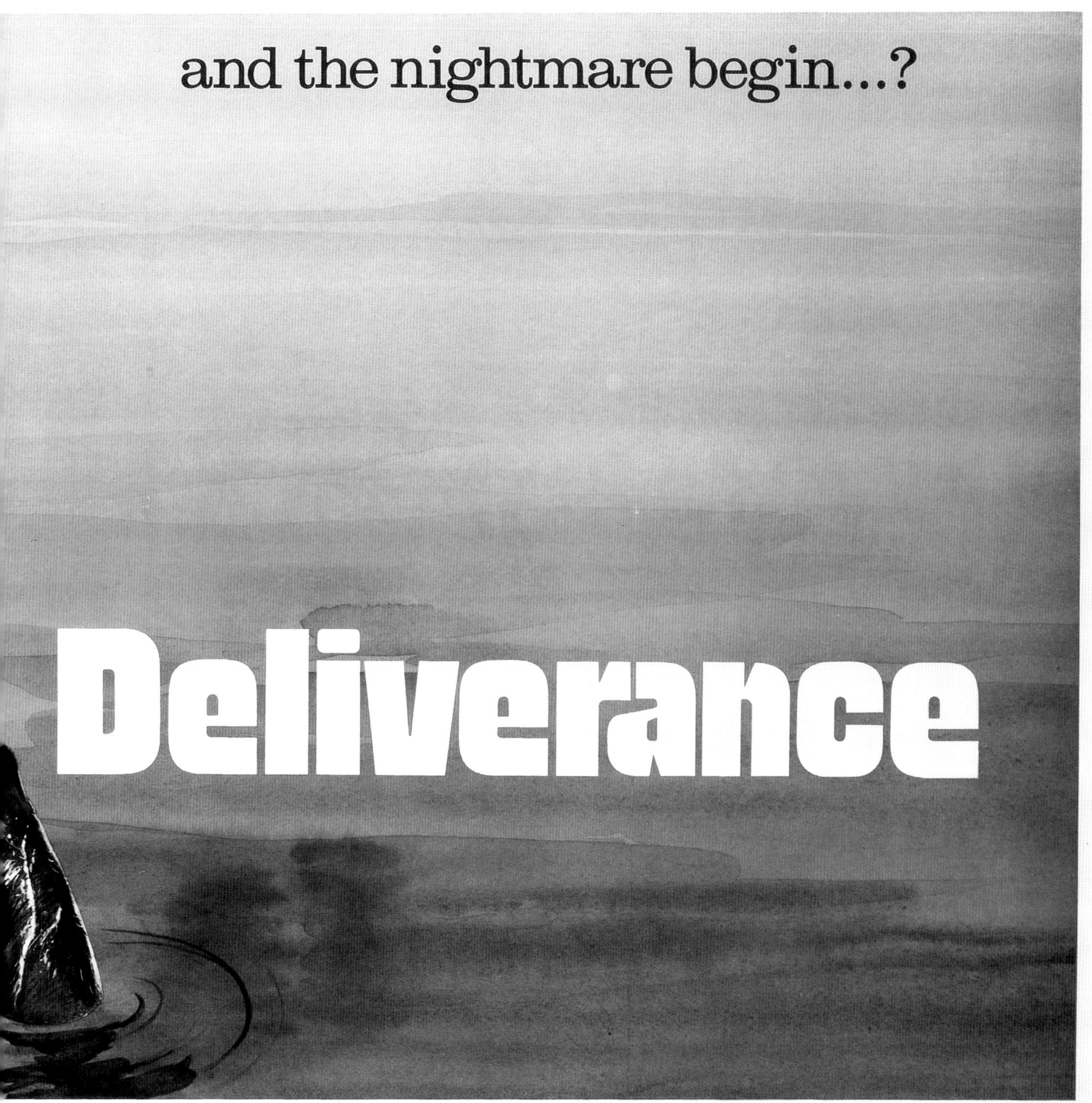
and the nightmare begin...?
Deliverance

IGHT · BURT REYNOLDS in "DELIVERANCE" X
ONNY COX · Screenplay by James Dickey Based on his novel · Produced and Directed by John Boorman
Warner Bros., A Warner Communications Company WB Released by Columbia-Warner Distributors Ltd.
PRINTED IN ENGLAND BY W. E. BERRY LTD. BRADFORD

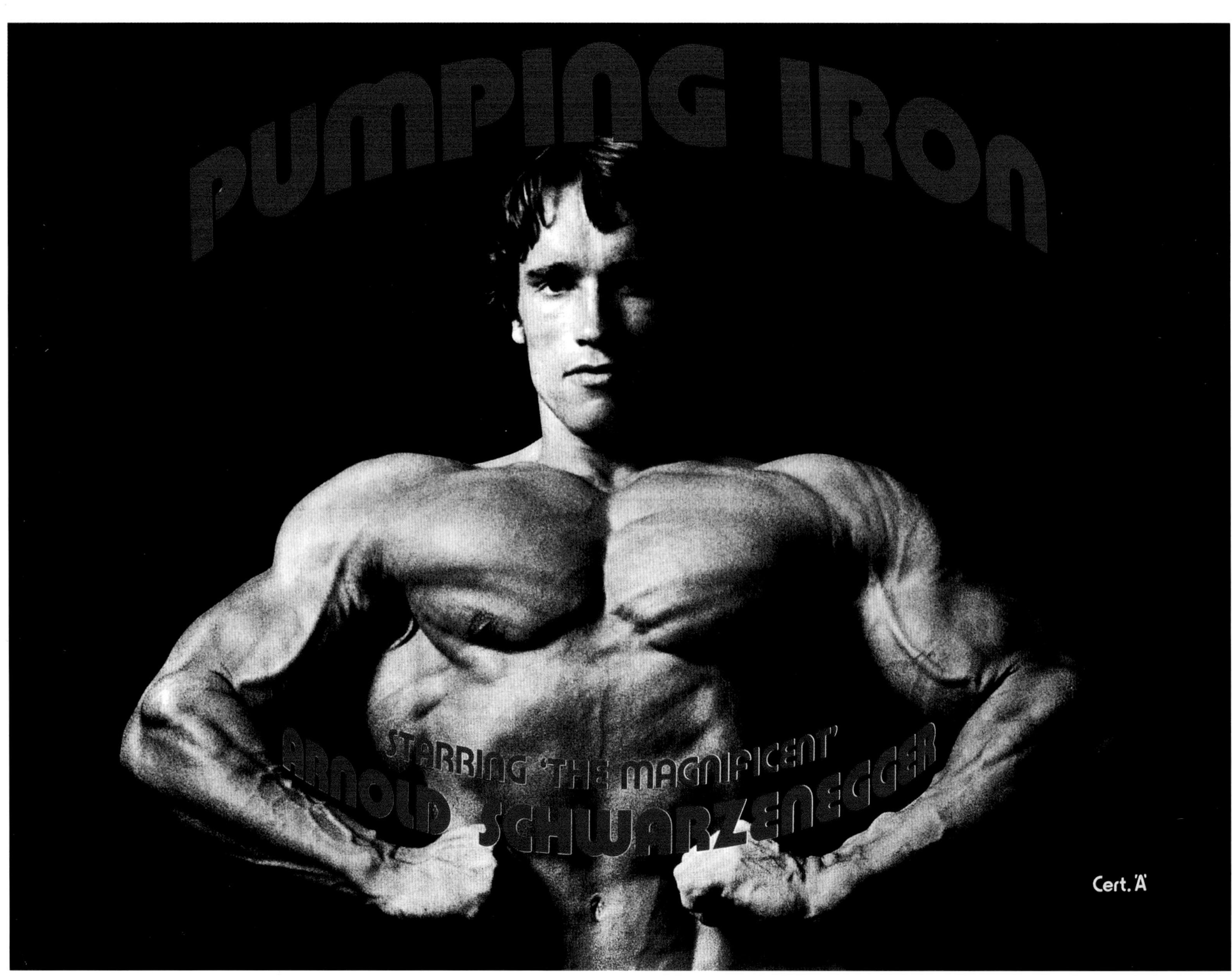

Pumping Iron (1977)
British 30 × 40 in. (76 × 102 cm)

Rocky (1976)
US 41 × 27 in. (104 × 69 cm)

His whole life was a million-to-one shot.

ROCKY

A ROBERT CHARTOFF-IRWIN WINKLER PRODUCTION · A JOHN G. AVILDSEN FILM · STARRING SYLVESTER STALLONE IN "ROCKY"

ALSO STARRING TALIA SHIRE · BURT YOUNG · CARL WEATHERS · AND BURGESS MEREDITH AS MICKEY · WRITTEN BY SYLVESTER STALLONE

PRODUCED BY IRWIN WINKLER AND ROBERT CHARTOFF · DIRECTED BY JOHN G. AVILDSEN · EXECUTIVE PRODUCER GENE KIRKWOOD · MUSIC BY BILL CONTI

PG PARENTAL GUIDANCE SUGGESTED
SOME MATERIAL MAY NOT BE SUITABLE FOR PRE-TEENAGERS

ORIGINAL MOTION PICTURE SOUNDTRACK ALBUM AND TAPE AVAILABLE ON UNITED ARTISTS UA RECORDS

United Artists
A Transamerica Company

77/2

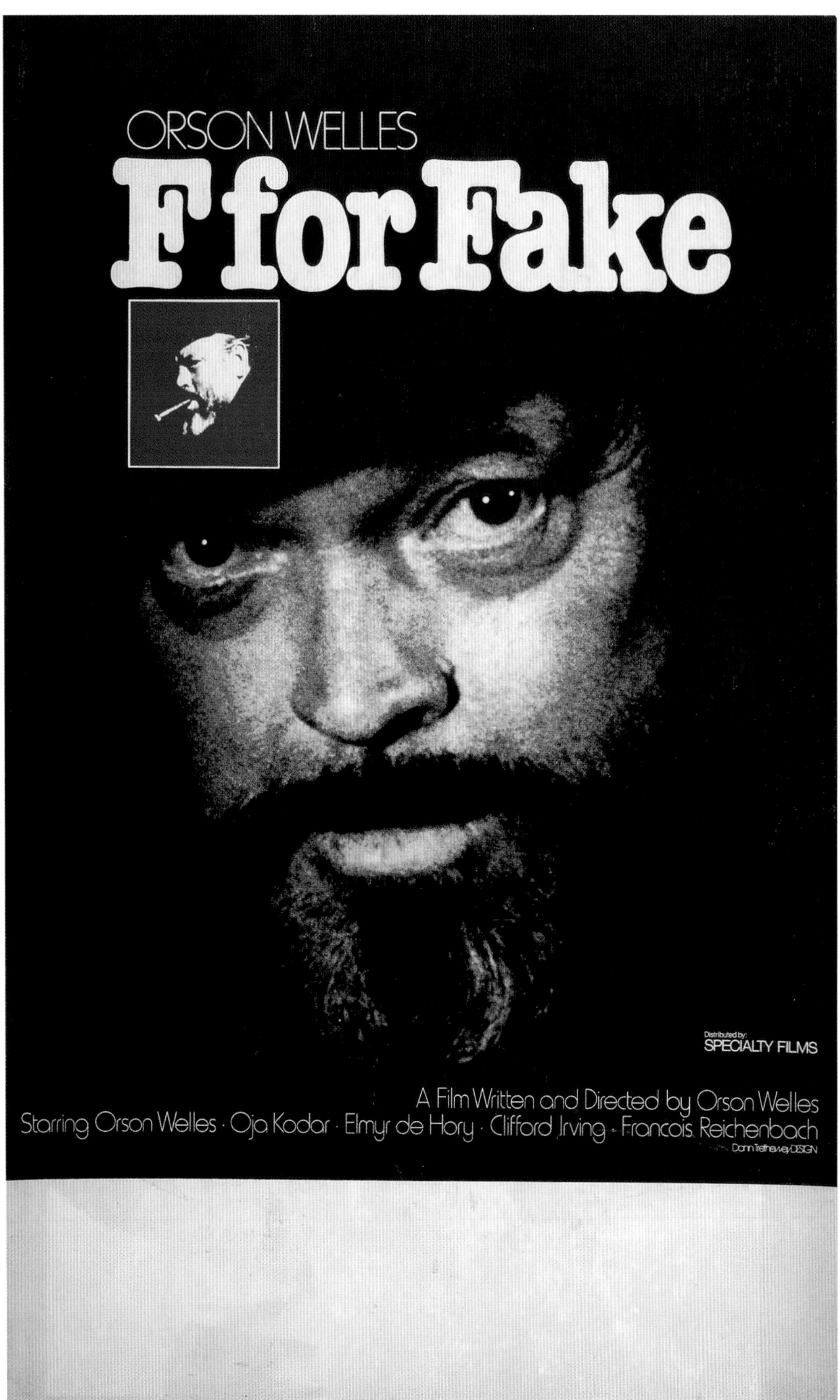

F For Fake (1973)
US 22 × 14 in. (56 × 36 cm)

The Candidate (1972)
US 41 × 27 in. (104 × 69 cm)
Art Director: Jeff Kanew

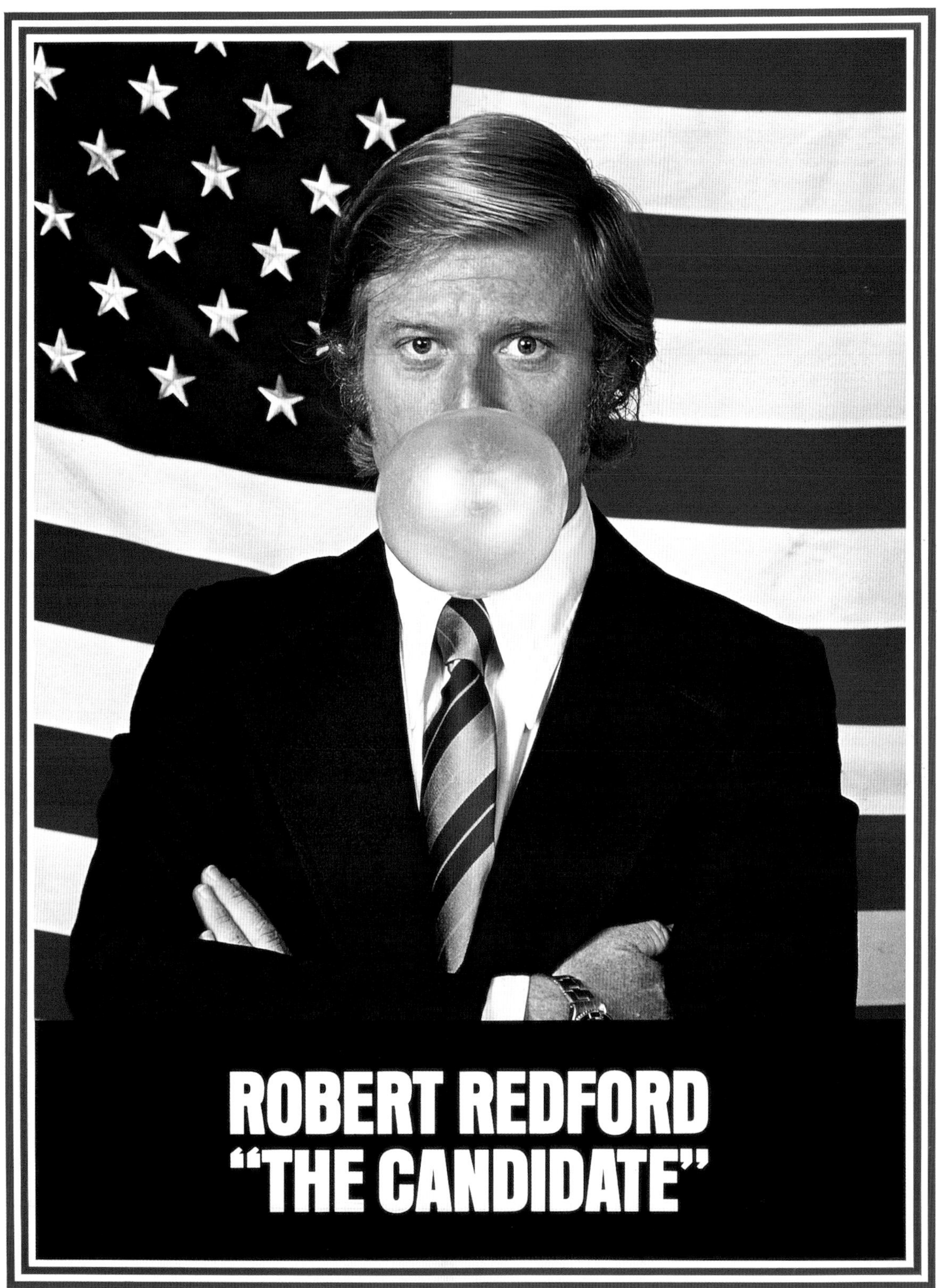

A WILDWOOD-RITCHIE PRODUCTION

ROBERT REDFORD in "THE CANDIDATE" Starring PETER BOYLE and MELVYN DOUGLAS as John J. McKay Directed by MICHAEL RITCHIE
Written by JEREMY LARNER Produced by WALTER COBLENZ TECHNICOLOR® From WARNER BROS. A WARNER COMMUNICATIONS COMPANY

PG PARENTAL GUIDANCE SUGGESTED

★★

This advertisement has been paid for by Warner Bros., who would love The Candidate to be a winner.

★★

72/235

ANNOUNCING

THE BREAKTHROUGH PRESENTATION OF STANLEY KUBRICK'S CLOCKWORK ORANGE FOR THE MILLIONS WHO WERE NOT ALLOWED TO SEE IT UNTIL NOW!

STANLEY KUBRICK'S

CLOCKWORK ORANGE

A Stanley Kubrick Production "A CLOCKWORK ORANGE" Starring Malcolm McDowell • Patrick Magee • Adrienne Corri and Miriam Karlin • Screenplay by Stanley Kubrick Based on the novel by Anthony Burgess • Produced and • Directed by Stanley Kubrick • Executive Producers Max L. Raab and Si Litvinoff • Original soundtrack available on Warner Bros. Records

From Warner Bros A Warner Communications Company

R RESTRICTED Under 17 requires accompanying Parent or Adult Guardian

index of film titles

A Clockwork Orange (1971)
US 41 × 27 in. (104 × 69 cm)
(Style B, R-Rated)

FILM POSTERS OF THE 60s

Film Posters of the 60s evokes the era when James Bond flicks were envelope-pushing fantasies for the bachelor-pad set.

NEWSWEEK

Here is a book which, for once, delivers just what you would expect from the title … For poster collectors – and everyone else – this is a crisp and stylish picture book.

DAILY MAIL